Chambers

Pocket Guide to Good English

Chambers
Pocket Guide to
Good English

Edited by George W. Davidson

Chambers

ISBN 0 550 18029 X

Printed by Mentor Printers Pte Ltd

Preface

Is 'data' singular or plural? How should one pronounce the word 'controversy'? Is it wrong to split infinitives? Is it correct to use 'hopefully' in the sense of 'I hope'? What is the difference between 'continual' and 'continuous', between 'infer' and 'imply', and between 'refute' and 'deny'? Most speakers of English have at some time or another asked questions like these, or have been asked them by someone else, but many people do not know where to find simple and straightforward answers to such questions. Now W & R Chambers, who have long had an international reputation as publishers of authoritative dictionaries of the English language, have produced this *Pocket Guide to Good English*, a concise and easy-to-use manual of modern English usage which provides the user with the clear, simple guidelines on grammar, vocabulary, spelling, pronunciation and punctuation which he or she needs in order to be able to write English confidently and correctly.

This book is not intended solely for students, secretaries, businessmen, and all those who in the course of their everyday work have to write reports, essays, letters or speeches. This book is for everyone who wants to speak and write English correctly. No home, office, or library should be without a copy of *Chambers Pocket Guide to Good English*.

Introduction

What is 'Good English'?

Everyone who speaks English knows that the plural of *book* is *books*, but that the plural of *man* is *men*, not *mans*. Similarly, the past tense of the verb *walk* is *walked*, but the past tense of *run* is *ran*, not *runned*. One has no choice in the matter: the rules of English grammar state that *men* and *ran* are correct, *mans* and *runned* incorrect. However, not all parts of the English language have quite as clear-cut rules as this. Sometimes there are two, or even more than two, possible ways of saying something, and a speaker or writer has to make a choice between these possibilities: in some cases, all the variant forms may be equally acceptable in all contexts; in other cases, one form may be generally considered more old-fashioned, more formal, or more colloquial than the other variants; and there are some points, such as the 'split infinitive', on which opinions are sharply divided and which are from time to time the subject of heated debates between speakers of English.

Throughout this book, the editor's aim in setting out rules and guidelines has been to steer a middle course between a too conservative clinging to out-dated usage and an uncritical approval of innovations whose acceptability has not yet been ascertained. No doubt some readers will feel that he has erred in being too cautious in his judgements, while others will criticize him for allowing what to them are heinous linguistic lapses: the editor was well aware from the outset that in writing a book such as this he could not expect all his recommendations to be accepted without dispute.

Obviously, a book of this size cannot hope to answer every question of grammar, style, etc. that might possibly arise, but must of necessity concentrate on the commonest and most troublesome points. However, although this is a concise guide to English usage, the editor has carefully avoided spurious over-simplification in the entries and has attempted throughout the book to give full and detailed information on the matters that are covered so that the reader will be certain to find the clear guidance on English usage that he or she is seeking. The editor will, of course, be pleased to answer any questions which readers find are not covered in this book, and will be grateful for any comments or suggestions readers care to send him.

How Information is Set Out in the *Pocket Guide*

Chambers Pocket Guide to Good English has been specifically designed for ease of use. The entries in the book are in alphabetical order, with the subject of each article clearly indicated in bold-face type (e.g. **abbreviations**; **flaunt, flout**; **seek**). When two or more words are dealt with in one article (e.g. **disinterested, uninterested**), the article is entered in the *Pocket Guide* at the alphabetical position of the first word, and cross-references are added where necessary (e.g. **uninterested** see **disinterested**) to indicate to the reader where he will find the information he is looking for.

Pronunciations are shown by phonetic symbols in square brackets, e.g. [*jāl*]. For a detailed chart of the symbols used, see page viii.

In most entries, the explanations are supplemented by idiomatic examples, and in a number of entries there are additional self-checking hints which will enable the reader to differentiate between correct and incorrect constructions which are especially difficult to distinguish. Throughout the book, common errors and incorrect constructions are marked by asterisks (thus ***acquiesce to**; ***stupidder**; ***He tried and came to the party**).

The emphasis in the *Pocket Guide to Good English* is on the English of the United Kingdom, but the editor has nonetheless indicated in various entries differences between British and American usage.

Finally, although this book has been so designed that readers can quickly find information on particular points of English usage when they need it, the editor would recommend that users also browse through this book at leisure—they may thus spot errors in their own usage that they would otherwise not even be aware of making.

Pronunciation guide

Accented syllables are shown by putting a stress mark after the accented syllable, thus *ban'dit, dis-pel', dis-gust'ing.*

Vowels and diphthongs

Sound		Examples	Pronunciation
ā	as in fate, bare	name, hair	*nām, hār*
ä	as in father, far	grass, harm	*gräs, härm*
a	as in sat	bad, have	*bad, hav*
ē	as in me, fear	lean, here	*lēn, hēr*
e	as in pet	red, said	*red, sed*
ə	as in dinner	river, above	*riv'ər, ə-buv'*
ī	as in mine, sire	side, hire	*sīd, hīr*
i	as in bid	pin, busy	*pin, biz'i*
ō	as in mote	bone	*bōn*
o	as in got	shot, shone	*shot, shon*
ōō	as in moon, poor	fool, tour	*fōōl, tōōr*
ŏŏ	as in foot	full, would	*fŏŏl, wŏŏd*
ū	as in mute, pure	tune, endure	*tūn, in-dūr*
u	as in bud	run, love	*run, luv*
û	as in her	heard, bird, world, absurd	*hûrd, bûrd, wûrld, əb-sûrd'*
oi	as in boy	buoy, soil	*boi, soil*

Consonants

b, d, f, h, j, k, l, m, n, p, r, s, t, v, w, and *z* are pronounced as in standard English.

The following other symbols are used:

Sound		Examples	Pronunciation
ch	as in cheap	church	*chûrch*
g	as in good	game	*gām*
sh	as in shine	shape, sugar	*shāp, shŏŏg'ər*
th	as in thin	theme, health	*thēm, helth*
dh	as in then	though, bathe	*dhō, bādh*
y	as in yet	yellow	*yel'ō*

a, an

The form **a** is used before words beginning with a consonant, as in *a road, a hospital, a yellow dress*. It is also used before words beginning with a vowel which is pronounced with a consonant sound, as in *a one-way street, a union*. The form **an** is used before words beginning with a vowel, as in *an axe, an egg, an orange skirt*. It is also used before words which begin with a vowel sound because the initial consonant is not pronounced, as in *an hour, an honour, an honest person*.

Since the choice of **a** or **an** depends on the pronunciation of the following word rather than on the written form of the word, the correct form to use before an abbreviation depends on the pronunciation of the abbreviation: if it begins with a consonant or consonant sound, it is preceded by **a,** as in *a BA, a UN peace-keeping force*; if it begins with a vowel or vowel sound, it is preceded by **an,** as in *an MA, an SOS, an IOU*.

a, an *after* no

A frequent error in English is the introduction of an unnecessary **a(n)** in constructions with **no** and a comparative adjective, as for example ** I can think of no worse a fate than that* and ** There is no more difficult a job than writing dictionaries*. The **a** in such sentences should be omitted, because here **no** is an adjective meaning 'not a' and modifies the following noun, as can be seen when the sentences are slightly rephrased: *I can think of no fate worse than that*; *There is no job more difficult than writing dictionaries*.

Expressions like this should be distinguished from the very similar construction seen in *His is no worse a job than mine*. Here the use of **a** is correct because **no** is an adverb, meaning 'not', modifying the following adjective, as can be seen when the sentence is rephrased: *His job is no worse than mine*.

If you are uncertain about whether or not to omit **a(n)** after **no** in a particular sentence, try rephrasing the sentence in the ways suggested above. This should help you to see whether **no** means 'not' or 'not a'.

abbreviations

Abbreviations are shortened forms of words, titles, phrases, etc. Abbreviations in English used always to be followed by full stops, but this is no longer so. Abbreviations which include the final letter of the word, such as *Mr* and *Dr*, and abbreviations of the names of countries and organizations, such as *USA, USSR, UN, EEC*, are now usually written without full stops, as are abbrevia-

1

tions of metric measurements, such as *km, cm, kg*. Other abbreviations are normally written with full stops, *ibid.* or *viz.* for example, but there is an increasing tendency to omit the full stops in these also: *e.g.* or *eg*, *i.e.* or *ie*.

Abbreviations of metric measurements do not add an *s* in the plural: *3 cm* (= 3 centimetres), *50 kg* (= 50 kilograms). With many non-metric measurements, forms with or without an *s* are equally acceptable: *3 lb* or *3 lbs* (= 3 pounds), *6 oz* or *6 ozs* (= 6 ounces), but in modern practice the *s* tends to be omitted. Certain abbreviations such as *cwt* (= hundredweight), *min.* (= minute) and *sec.* (= second) never take an *s* in the plural.

abide

When this verb is used in the phrase **abide by** (= to act according to, be faithful to), the past tense and past participle are **abided:** *He said he would abide by our decision and he has abided by it.* However, when **abide** is used in the archaic or literary sense of 'to live', the past tense and past participle are **abode:** *She abode by a lake.*

-able, -ible

The suffix **-able** is used to form adjectives from verbs and some nouns, e.g.

adaptable	*indispensable*	*reliable*
detachable	*indefinable*	*respectable*
debatable	*likeable*	*sizeable*
fashionable	*payable*	*usable*

When **-able** is added to a word ending in *e*, the *e* is normally dropped:

advise	:	*advisable*	*define*	:	*indefinable*
debate	:	*debatable*	*mistake*	:	*unmistakable*

There are, however, exceptions to this rule:

1. If the word ends in *-ce* or *-ge*, the *e* is not dropped:

change : *changeable* *notice* : *noticeable*

2. There are a number of words, mostly ones derived from short verbs, in which the *e* is normally retained. Among these are *blameable, likeable, rateable, sizeable*.

In the case of verbs whose final consonant is doubled in the formation of the present participle, the final consonant is similarly doubled in forming **-able** adjectives:

bid	:	*bidding*	:	*biddable*
forget	:	*forgetting*	:	*unforgettable*

Exceptions to this rule are verbs ending in *-fer*, which do not double the final *r* before **-able:**

prefer	: *preferring*	: *preferable*
transfer	: *transferring*	: *transferable*

Where a verb ends in *-y* preceded by a consonant, the *y* changes to *i* before **-able:**

justify : *justifiable* but *pay* : *payable*

(*flyable* is an exception to this rule).

Some adjectives end in the suffix **-ible** rather than **-able** because they follow the form of the Latin words from which they are derived. There is a great deal of confusion in English about this, and many words ending in **-able** and **-ible** are misspelt. Common adjectives in **-ible** include:

audible	*feasible*	*permissible*
comprehensible	*flexible*	*reversible*
credible	*gullible*	*sensible*
edible	*legible*	*susceptible*
eligible	*negligible*	*visible*

Nouns formed from adjectives ending in **-able** and **-ible** end in **-ability** and **-ibility** respectively:

adaptable : *adaptability*   *eligible* : *eligibility*

about see **around.**

about to see **going to.**

above, over, on top (of)

Above, over, and **on top (of)** are all used to describe the position of something relative to some other thing which is at a lower level than it. Speakers of English, however, are not always clear about the differences in meaning between these words.

On top (of) is used when the things concerned are touching one another: *He piled the books one on top of the other; a large plate of ice-cream with a cherry on top.*

Over also can be used when the things under discussion are touching, but carries the further implication of one thing covering the other: *an apple tart with custard over it; He was carrying his jacket over his arm.* When the things are not in contact with each other, there is still an implication of a close, direct link between them, especially of one thing being directly above the other thing or passing from one side of it to the other side: *He held an umbrella over them; He jumped over the gate.*

Above may, like **over,** be used when one thing is directly above the other, as in *Hang the picture over/above the bookcase*, but often suggests a less direct or close relationship between the things

3

concerned than is implied by **over:** *He could see the climbers high up on the mountains above him* (i.e. the climbers and mountains were higher than him, but not directly overhead).

When **over** and **above** are used figuratively to describe people's relative importance or seniority, **over** again marks a closer relationship than **above:** if Mr Smith is *above* Mr Brown, he is simply more important than him or senior to him; but if Mr Smith is *over* Mr Brown, he is not only senior to Mr Brown but also has authority over him.

abridgement, abridgment

May be spelt with or without the *e*. The spelling with the *e* is the commoner.

abscess

This word is frequently misspelt. Note the *sc* in the middle of the word, and *ss* at the end.

abuse, misuse

The verbs **abuse** and **misuse** both mean 'to use (something) in an incorrect way'. These verbs do, however, differ slightly in meaning and use.

Misuse refers mostly to the use of solid things or objects in an incorrect way or in a way in which they were not intended to be used. This wrong use may not be deliberate, but rather caused by ignorance. The results are usually, but not always, harmful or undesirable: *This drill has been misused and will not work properly now*; *The Treasurer was accused of misusing the club's money.* Sometimes **misuse** is used to refer to the wrong use of more abstract things such as words, powers, or laws: *Giving that money to charity was misusing your powers as Treasurer.*

Abuse refers most often to the incorrect use of abstract things, especially one's position, power or privileges, in a way that is considered bad, harmful, or immoral: *To use the club's money to buy yourself a car would be abusing your position as Treasurer.* **Abuse** is now only rarely used to refer to the wrong use or mishandling of solid objects, such as tools, equipment or machinery.

The above distinctions apply equally to the nouns **abuse** and **misuse.**

accommodation

A word frequently misspelt. It has two *c*'s and two *m*'s.

account

The verb **account** is followed by the preposition **for** when it means 'to give a (satisfactory) reason for', as in *He could not account for his strange behaviour.* When **account** means 'to consider', it has no preposition after it, and is often found in the passive voice, as in *He was accounted a good pianist.* This use is rather formal.

The adjective **accountable** is followed by the prepositions **to** and **for,** as in *He is accountable to me for his actions.*

acknowledgement, acknowledgment

May be spelt with or without the *e*. The form with the *e* is the commoner.

acquaint, acquainted

Acquaint and **acquainted** should be followed by the preposition **with,** as in *Have you acquainted yourself with the layout of the building?*; *Are you acquainted with her father?* To **acquaint** (someone) **with** (information, plans, etc.) is a rather formal substitute for 'tell' or 'inform', and *acquaint someone with the facts* is felt by some people to be a cliché which should be avoided if possible.

acquiesce

This word is frequently misspelt. Note the *cqu* and the *sc*.

The verb **acquiesce** may be used on its own, meaning 'to agree', as in *After much persuasion, he finally acquiesced.* It may also be followed by the preposition **in,** as in *He acquiesced in our suggestions.* **Acquiesce** and **acquiesce in** are mostly used in formal or literary speech and writing; **agree** and **agree to** are more usual in informal contexts.

****Acquiesce to** is incorrect, and probably arises from a confusion between **agree to** and **acquiesce in.**

-acy, -asy

Words ending in **-acy** and **-asy** are often misspelt, *s* being written where *c* is correct and vice versa.

The ending **-acy** is the commoner of the two. Among words ending in **-acy** are:

aristocracy	*bureaucracy*	*intimacy*	*privacy*
autocracy	*celibacy*	*obstinacy*	

Some common words ending in **-asy** are:

apostasy	*ecstasy*	*idiosyncrasy*

If you are uncertain about the correct spelling of a word not on these lists, consult a dictionary.

(Note that the words ending in **-cracy** are related to words ending in **-crat:** *aristocrat, bureaucrat,* etc. This provides a useful rule of thumb which helps with at least some of the spelling problems.)

adherence, adhesion

Both of these words convey the notion of 'sticking to' something, but differ slightly in use. **Adhesion** is used more often when what is being described is one thing literally sticking to another, as in *Which brand of glue gives the best adhesion?* **Adherence,** on the other hand, is generally used to refer to a person's 'sticking to' something in a more figurative sense, such as one's remaining faithful to one's beliefs or belonging to a political party: *his adherence to communism; his adherence to the Liberal Party.*

adjacent, adjoining, contiguous

The adjective **adjacent** means 'close to, next to, beside': *the house adjacent to mine; adjacent fields.* Although beside each other, things which are adjacent are not necessarily touching or in contact with each other: *adjacent rooms* in a building may only be separated by the wall between them, but *adjacent houses* may be separated by gardens, garages, etc.

Adjoining means 'next to and touching'. *Adjacent houses* may have gardens between them, but *adjoining houses* will be separated by nothing more than the wall between them. *Adjoining* very often carries the further implication of there being direct access from one thing to the other: *adjoining rooms* may have a door between them, *adjoining fields* a gate through which one can pass from one field to the other.

Contiguous, like **adjoining,** means 'next to and touching, having an edge or boundary in common'. It is generally found in formal or technical contexts. **Contiguous** may be followed by **to** or, less frequently, **with:** *Name any country contiguous to Pakistan.*

adjoining see adjacent.

admission, admittance

Admittance means 'the act of entering, the right to enter, permission to enter' a place, especially a place not generally open to the public, such as a house or factory. The word occurs most frequently in such phrases as *no admittance* or *to gain admittance.*

Admission also means 'the act of entering, permission to enter', but is more often used when one is referring either to entry into a public place such as a theatre or cinema, or to the price or conditions of entry, as in *Admission £1; Admission by ticket only; No admission after 10 o'clock.* **Admission** is also used for entry into a club or society, or into a school (as a pupil) or hospital (as a patient).

Admission also means 'confession, acknowledgement', as *an admission of guilt.*

admit

To **admit** something is 'to say that one recognizes or accepts the truth of' it: *He admitted that he had been wrong.* It also means 'to confess': *He admitted his guilt; He admitted that he had stolen the money; He admitted stealing the money.* A third meaning of **admit,** 'to describe, confide (one's thoughts or feelings)' can be seen in *He admitted feeling rather ashamed.*

In the senses of 'confess' and 'confide', **admit** may be followed by the preposition **to:** *He admitted to having stolen the money*; *I must admit to having felt thoroughly ashamed of myself.*

Admit of is a rather formal expression meaning 'to allow', as in *The rules admit of no exceptions; This admits of no other explanation.* The subject of the verb in this construction must always be impersonal or abstract, as in the examples above: **He admits of no exceptions* is incorrect (say, rather, *He allows no exceptions*).

admittance see admission.

adverse, averse

Adverse means 'unfavourable, hostile, harmful', as in *adverse weather conditions; adverse criticism.* It is more often applied to things than people, and is sometimes followed by the preposition **to** in formal speech and writing: *Such carelessness is adverse to the success of our project.*

Averse means 'having a dislike, disinclined', and is followed by **to** or, less frequently, **from:** *I'm not averse to hard work.* **Averse** cannot immediately precede the noun it modifies: one may say *Though averse to hard work, he agreed to help* or *His friends are as averse to hard work as he is,* but one cannot talk of **his averse friends* or **averse feelings.*

advice, advise

The word **advice** is a noun: *She asked her mother's advice on/about what she should wear to the meeting.*

Advice is sometimes confused with **advise,** which is a verb meaning 'to give advice to', as in *Her mother advised her on what to wear.* Note the difference between *He advised me to buy the house* (= he said I should buy it) and *He advised me on buying the house* (he told me how to buy it).

Advise is also used in formal English with the meaning 'to inform', and is followed by the preposition **of,** as in *You should advise your lawyer of your complaint against the firm,* or by **that,** as in *I have to advise you that a complaint has been made about your behaviour.*

In business contexts only, **advise** is sometimes used without **of,** as in *Please advise the date of delivery*, but the use of the **of-** construction is obligatory in other contexts.

aeroplane, airplane, plane, aircraft

Aeroplane is the British English form of this word, **airplane** the normal form in American English. Although in origin an abbreviation, **plane** is now considered a complete word and should not be written with an apostrophe (*'*plane*).

Aircraft is a more technical word than **aeroplane,** and is wider in meaning, including not only aeroplanes, but also helicopters, gliders, airships, etc. The plural of **aircraft** is **aircraft.**

affect, effect

Affect and **effect** are often confused. **Affect** is a verb meaning 'to have an influence on, to cause a change in', as in *Your answer will not affect my decision; The accident has affected his eyesight.* **Effect** can be used both as a noun and a verb. As a verb, it is rather formal, and means 'to cause, bring about', as in *He tried to effect a reconciliation between his parents.* As a noun, **effect** means 'result, consequence, impression', as in *He has recovered from the effects of his illness; Your action will have little effect on him.*

affinity

All authorities agree that this word should be followed by **between** or **with,** as in *the affinity between French and Spanish; the affinity of Brown's philosophy with that of Plato; the affinity that exists between friends.*

When **affinity** is used in the sense of 'closeness in relationship or form', it is sometimes followed by the preposition **to.** This construction is not, however, considered correct by most authorities and although quite common in informal English, is best avoided in formal speech or writing.

When used with the meaning 'liking' or 'attraction', **affinity** is often followed by **for** or **to,** as in *He has a great affinity for cats.* Although this construction is common in informal English, it is still disapproved of by many people, and should not be used in formal English. The one exception to this is in scientific writing, in which **affinity for** may correctly be used in describing the readiness with which one chemical unites with another: *The haemoglobin in blood has a great affinity for oxygen.*

afflict, inflict

The rather formal or literary verb **afflict** means 'to cause great pain or distress to'. It may be followed by the preposition **with,** as in *They believed that it was God who had afflicted them with a plague of rats*. **Afflict** is most often used in the passive, followed by **with** or **by**: *He is afflicted with/by headaches*. When one wishes to refer to an action, event, or onset of a condition rather than to a continuing state, **by** rather than **with** should be used: *He was afflicted by the news of his wife's death*.

Inflict, which is sometimes confused with **afflict,** means 'to impose (something unpleasant or unwanted)' on someone. The confusion between **afflict** and **inflict** doubtless arises from their similarity in sound and meaning, but the constructions following these two verbs are quite different: one **afflicts** some<u>one</u> **with** some<u>thing</u>, but one **inflicts** some<u>thing</u> **on** some<u>one</u>, as in *They inflicted heavy casualties on the enemy.*

afraid

The adjective **afraid** may be followed by the prepositions **of** or **to.** When what follows is a noun, the correct preposition to use is **of:** *The little boy was afraid of dogs; He is afraid of the dark*. When what follows is a verb, either **of** or **to** can be used: *She is afraid of meeting him*; *She is afraid to go*. There is, however, an important difference in meaning between these two constructions. **Afraid to** is used when there is real fear involved, fear which prevents one doing something: *She is afraid to tell the manager what she thinks of him*. **Afraid of** also may be used when a feeling of fear is implied, especially fear of something happening to one, as in *He is afraid of losing his job*, but is also used when reluctance or concern rather than fear is implied, as in *She didn't go into the room as she was afraid of wakening the baby* (i.e. she was not frightened by the thought of the baby being wakened, she simply didn't want to waken it).

agenda

Although in origin a plural Latin noun, this word is singular in English: *We'll have to draw up an agenda for the meeting*. The plural is **agendas.**

aggravate

The original meaning of the word **aggravate** is 'to make worse', as in *His bad temper aggravated the situation*, but **aggravate** is also used with the meaning 'to annoy, irritate', as in *Loud music always aggravates her*. This latter meaning of **aggravate** is quite acceptable, and very common, in informal English, and although it is still regarded as incorrect by some people, it is now so well established, especially in the adjective form **aggravating,** that it cannot justifiably be condemned even in formal or literary English.

aghast

This word is sometimes misspelt. Note the *h* after the *g*.

ago, since

These two words are often used together, as in *It is months ago since I last met her.* This use is incorrect and should be avoided. Either use **since** or **ago** alone, as in *It is months since I last met her* or *I last met her months ago,* or use **ago** followed by **that,** as in *It was months ago that I last met her.*

agree

The verb **agree** can be followed by **on, to,** or **with,** depending on the meaning. It is followed by **with** when it means 'to think or say the same as', as in *I agree with them,* or when it means 'to be good for', as in *The climate agrees with his health* or *Coffee doesn't agree with me.* **Agree** is followed by **on** when it means 'to discuss and come to a decision about', as in *We agreed on a date for the next meeting.* Followed by **to,** it means that a person will do or allow something, as in *The teacher has agreed to our request; He agreed to come.*

Agree is quite frequently found in present-day English without a following preposition when used in the senses of **agree on** and **agree to:** *We agreed a price; We agreed their plan.* This construction is still condemned by some, but is now generally accepted as correct.

aim

Aim meaning 'to plan, intend' may be followed by either **at** or **to,** but the verb-forms following these two prepositions are different and care should be taken to select the correct one. One must say either *He aims to finish the job tomorrow* or *He aims at finishing the job tomorrow.*

When it means 'to point (something) at, to try to hit or reach (something)', **aim** may be followed by **at** or **for,** as in *He aimed at the target; He aimed for their legs; He is aiming at a seat on the council; She was aiming for the top in her career.*

aircraft, airplane see **aeroplane.**

alibi

Alibi is a Latin word meaning 'somewhere else'. It is correctly used in English to refer to one form of defence against a criminal charge, the defence being that the accused person was 'somewhere else' (i.e. not at the scene of the crime) when the crime was committed. In present-day English, however, **alibi** is often used to mean 'an excuse for not having done something'. This looser use of the word **alibi,** while fairly common in informal speech, is not yet accepted as correct by many people, and should therefore be avoided in careful or formal English.

all

The word **all** is followed by the preposition **of** if it is used to describe a following personal pronoun, as in *All of us want to go.* When **all** describes a demonstrative word such as *this* or *that* and a noun referring to a particular thing or things, specific people, etc., **of** is optional: *All the boys came* and *All of the boys came* are both correct as are *He ate all the cheese*, and *He ate all of the cheese*, and *All these are mine* and *All of these are mine.* When the noun refers to some general category of thing, person, etc., **all** may not be followed by **of:** *All men must die*; *All dogs must be kept on a lead.*

When the noun or pronoun described by **all** is the subject of the sentence, **all** may follow the noun or pronoun or verbs such as *can*, *will*, *may*, *must*, etc.: *We all want to go*; *We can all go*; *The boys all came*; *The boys must all come.*

all right, alright

Although appearing with increasing frequency in present-day English, *alright is not yet a generally accepted spelling of **all right.** At present the only correct form is **all right.**

all together see altogether.

allusion see delusion.

alright see all right.

also, as well, too

Too and **as well** are less formal than **also.** Many speakers of English therefore prefer to use **too** or **as well** when speaking informally, since the use of **also** might sound rather stilted or inappropriately formal.

Care must be taken to position **also, too** and **as well** correctly in a sentence. **Too** and **as well** follow the word to which they refer: *He gave me food, and money too/as well.* **Also** usually precedes the word it refers to, as in *He gave me food, and also money,* but follows the word if it is the subject of the sentence: *He also gave me food and money* (i.e. he as well as others). However, **also, too** and **as well** need not stand next to the words they refer to: in the sentence *He gave food to me too,* **too** may refer to *he, gave, food* or *me,* and the sentence may therefore be interpreted in four different ways.

Notice that after a negative word like **not**, **also**, etc. are generally replaced by **either**: *He didn't give me any food either.*

alternate, alternative

The adjective **alternate** refers either to something happening, coming, etc. in turns, one after the other, as in *The water came in alternate bursts of hot and cold* (i.e. first hot, then cold, then hot, then cold, and so on), or to something which happens, comes, etc. every second day, week, year, etc., as in *He visits us on alternate Tuesdays*. **Alternative** refers to the offering of a choice between two possibilities (or sometimes more than than two – see the following article): *an alternative plan.*

The same distinctions in meaning apply to the adverbs **alternately** and **alternatively**: *The water ran alternately hot and cold; They could go by bus, or alternatively they could take the train.*

alternative

The word **alternative,** as a noun or adjective, originally referred to one of two choices: *An alternative (arrangement) can be found if this plan doesn't suit you.* It is frequently used in present-day English to refer to one of more than two choices, although some people still regard this as incorrect: *We are using this method because all the alternatives (or all the alternative methods) have failed; We have only three alternatives.* If one wishes to avoid this use of **alternative**, one may use an adjective such as **other** and nouns such as **choice** or **option**: *We are using this method because all (the) other methods have failed; We have only three options.*

altogether, all together

Altogether means 'completely', 'in total', or 'all things considered': *I'm not altogether satisfied with your work*; *Altogether, we've collected £500; I'm wet, I'm tired and I'm cold. In fact, altogether I'm feeling pretty miserable.* **All together** means 'all in a group in one place', as in *I'll put these books all together on the shelf.* **All together** can be separated by other words, as in *I'll put all these books together on the shelf*; **altogether** is a single word and can never be split.

ambiguous, ambivalent

Both these words refer to a situation in which there exists a degree of uncertainty, but their meanings should not be confused. **Ambiguous** means 'having more than one possible meaning': *'After the cat caught the mouse, it died' is an ambiguous sentence because it is not clear whether 'it' refers to the cat or the mouse.* **Ambivalent** means 'having mixed feelings or emotions' about something, and may be followed by **toward(s)** or **about:** *Most of the staff are ambivalent towards John's promotion; ambivalent feelings.*

amend, emend

These two words are frequently confused because their meanings are very similar. To **amend** something is to alter, improve, or correct it: *We shall amend the error as soon as possible; We wish to amend the law/constitution.* **Emend** means specifically 'to correct the errors in' a book or other piece of writing: *We will emend your manuscript where necessary.*

The noun from **amend** is **amendment.** The noun from **emend** is **emendation.**

American spelling

There are a number of differences between the spelling of words in American English and that of British English. Some of the most important of these are listed below:

1.   Some verbs, especially those ending in *l* and *p*, which in British English double their final consonant before *-ing, -ed* and *-er/-or* do not do so in American English: for example, British English *travelling, kidnapped, equalled, counsellor,* but American *traveling, kidnaped, equaled, counselor.* This applies to certain nouns and adjectives also: note for example the normal American spellings *carburetor* (British *carburettor*) and *woolen* (British *woollen*).

2.   With verbs that may be spelt *-ise* or *-ize,* Americans prefer *-ize.*

3.   Most words which in British English end in *-our* end in *-or* in American English, e.g. *color, humor.*

4.   Many words which in British English end in *-re* are spelt *-er* by Americans: *center, theater, fiber, specter, meager.* Exceptions to this are generally words ending in *-cre* or *-gre*: *acre, massacre, ogre* are correct in both British and American English.

5.   The tendency to replace *ae* and *oe* in words from Greek and Latin by *e* is more strongly developed in the United States than in Britain: *haemoglobin, encyclopaedia, diarrhoea,* are normal in British English, *hemoglobin, encyclopedia, diarrhea,* usual in American English.

6.   Among the other words which are spelt differently in American English are *axe* (Amer. *ax*), *catalogue* (Amer. *catalog*), *cheque* (Amer. *check*), *plough* (Amer. *plow*), *programme* (Amer. *program*) and *sceptic* (Amer. *skeptic*).

amiable, amicable

Amiable means 'friendly, pleasant, good-natured' and is normally used of people, facial expressions, personalities, etc.: *John is a very amiable young man; an amiable smile.*

Amicable is generally used when referring to arrangements, agreements or discussions, and means 'done in a friendly way, showing goodwill'. When applied to people, **amicable** refers to their friendly behaviour or attitude on a particular occasion rather than to their general personality: *We don't usually get on well together but she was quite amicable at the party last night.*

among, amongst

Among is now far commoner than **amongst**.

For the difference between **among** and **between**, see **between**.

amoral see immoral.

an see a.

-ance, -ant, -ence, -ent

The choice of *a* or *e* in words like *dependent, relevant, inhabitant*, etc. is one which causes many people a great deal of trouble, and there are virtually no easy-to-learn general rules to assist one with the correct choice. Words in which the second last syllable is *-fer-*, *-isc-/-esc-*, or *-sist-* usually have *-ence/-ent*: *circumference, conference, difference, preference, adolescent, convalescent, fluorescent, reminiscent, consistent, persistent, subsistence*, but note *resistance*; words which are related to verbs ending in *-ate* or nouns in *-ation* take *-ance/-ant*: *lubricate, lubricant; migrate, migrant; participate, participant; radiate, radiance; variation, variant.*

Beyond these few guidelines, one is obliged simply to learn by rote. Among the commoner words ending in *-ance/-ant* are *abundance, acquaintance, appearance, attendant, constant, contestant, exuberant, extravagant, grievance, hindrance, inhabitant, informant, maintenance, nuisance, relevant, vagrant, vengeance*. Among the words ending with *-ence/-ent* are *apparent, competent, continent, correspondent, eminent, existence, experience, innocent, intelligent, experience, innocent, intelligent, negligent, occurrence, permanent, repellent, reverent, superintendent, sentence.* Note also *tendency.*

A small number of words present a particular problem in that their spelling varies according to whether they are nouns or adjectives: *dependant, descendant, pendant* and *propellant* are nouns; *dependent, propellent*, etc. are adjectives. (Note, however, that *independent* is the correct form for both the noun and the adjective.)

angry

The adjective **angry** may be followed by the prepositions **about, at, over** or **with**.

When the anger is directed at people, **angry** is normally followed by **with**, as in *She was angry with me for dropping the cups*. **Angry at** is also correct when referring to people, as in *She got angry at me when I laughed at her*, but is less common than **angry with**.

When referring to actions or things, **angry** is normally followed by **about, at,** or **over**. **At** is sometimes preferred to **about** and **over** when what is being referred to is the feeling of anger arising at the time of the action which causes the anger rather than anger felt later on: compare, for example, *I got really angry at his remarks yesterday* (i.e. the anger immediately followed his remarks) and *I feel really angry about what he said yesterday* (i.e. the remarks were made yesterday, but I still feel angry today).

animal, beast

Animal is the more usual word: *Dogs and cats are animals*. **Beast** is a rather more formal word, used especially to refer to large, often fierce, animals: *the beasts of the jungle*. The word **beast** is also found in the phrase *beast of burden* (= an animal used for carrying loads), now used mainly in literary and figurative contexts.

annual, perennial

Annual means 'happening once every year', as in *The flower-show is an annual event*, or 'of one year', as in *What is his annual salary?* When applied to plants, **annual** means 'lasting for only one year' or, as a noun 'a plant which lives for only one year'.

Perennial originally means 'lasting or continuing through the year', but is now used, mostly in formal or facetious contexts, in the sense of 'perpetual', 'continual' or 'recurrent': *I'm tired of listening to her perennial complaints*; *a perennial problem*. When used of plants, **perennial** means '(a plant) which last for more than two years'.

See also the article **biennial, biannual**.

ante-, anti-

The similarity in spelling and pronunciation between these two prefixes may lead to their being confused with each other.

Ante- means 'before', as in *antenatal* 'before birth', and *anteroom* 'a room opening into another, more important, room'.

Anti- means 'against' or 'opposite', as in *anti-aircraft gun*, *antibiotic* 'a medicine used against bacteria', *anticlockwise*, etc.

anticipate

The verb **anticipate** is often used with the meaning 'to foresee (something) and take action to prevent it, counter it, meet its requirements, etc.', as in *He's an excellent chess-player — he anticipated every move I made* or *A good businessman must try to anticipate his customers' requirements.*

Some people still consider this to be the only correct meaning of **anticipate,** but for most speakers of English this verb has another meaning, equivalent simply to 'foresee' or 'expect': *The police said that they were not anticipating any trouble from the strikers.* Although it is perhaps unfortunate that **anticipate** has taken on this wider meaning – in some contexts, it may not be clear whether one is merely expecting something or both expecting it and taking some action with regard to it – this use of the verb is so firmly established and widely accepted now that it cannot any longer be condemned as incorrect. However, care should be taken, especially in writing, to avoid any confusion that might possibly arise from the use of this now ambiguous verb.

apostrophe

I Deletions

An apostrophe is often used to show that one or more letters or figures have been omitted from a word or number: *can't* is an abbreviation of *cannot*, *it's* of *it is*, *she'll* of *she will*, *I'd* of *I had* or *I would*, *the '30s* of *the 1930s*. Note that many words which are in origin abbreviations of longer words are now no longer written with apostrophes: *bus, flu, phone, plane.*

II Possessives

A further use of the apostrophe is seen in the formation of possessive nouns. The general rules which apply to the use of apostrophes with possessives are quite straightforward, but there are a few important exceptions to these rules which also must be noted. The basic rules are as follows:

The possessive form of a noun is shown, in writing, by the addition of *'s*, as in *the child's dog; the children's dog; James's dog; Robert Burns's dog.*

If the noun is plural and already ends in *s*, the apostrophe alone is used: *the boys' dog*, not **the boys's dog*. This applies also to certain expressions of time in which the time expression is treated as a possessive: *He's coming in two weeks' time.*

Notice that in all these cases, the written form of the words mirrors the spoken form: where an additional *s* is pronounced in a spoken possessive form, it is added in the written form; where no *s* is added in pronunciation, the apostrophe alone is added on the written form.

In a few exceptional cases, a singular noun ending in *s* is followed by an apostrophe alone rather than by *'s*. However, the existence of such exceptions to the general rule will not give rise to any confusion or uncertainty if it is remembered that, in such cases also, the correct written form of the words reflects the pronunciation of the spoken form. In other words, if you pronounce the possessive *'s*, write it; if you don't pronounce an *s*, don't write one. The main exceptions are names whose pronunciation with an additional *s* would be difficult or clumsy: *If you compare these two cars, you'll find that the Mercedes' engine is the more powerful.* Biblical and ancient Greek and Roman names which end in *s* can also be treated in this way, as in *Moses' laws, Xerxes' army,* but although still correct, this is not as prevalent as it used to be.

It should be noted that in certain expressions with **sake,** nouns ending in an *s* sound which by the nature of the construction ought to end in *'s* are now usually written without even an apostrophe: compare *for heaven's sake* and *for goodness sake.*

Do not use an apostrophe with possessive pronouns: the correct forms are *yours, hers, its* (*it's* = *it is*), *ours, theirs. One's,* however, is correct. Note also the possessive form *whose,* not **who's* (*who's* = *who is*).

III Plurals

Apostrophes should not normally be used in the formation of plural nouns: plural forms such as **book's,* **bag's,* **lolly's* are increasingly common, and care should be taken to avoid them. An apostrophe is, however, permitted in plurals in a few specific cases, mainly for the sake of clarity:

1. An apostrophe is frequently written in the plurals of a number of, mostly short, words such as *do* (as in *do's and don'ts*), *me* (as *I feel there are two me's at the moment*), *set-to* (as *I've had a few set-to's with him*), *he* and *she* (as in *Are the puppies he's or she's?*), but *dos, set-tos, hes* and *shes* are equally possible (*mes* seems less acceptable than *hes* and *shes,* for no obvious reason).

2. When the word in the plural is the title of a book, play, etc *'s* is often used instead of *s* alone: *There have been three Macbeth's* (= three different versions of the play 'Macbeth') *performed in Edinburgh in the past six months,* but here again, *s* alone is equally permissible. *'s,* rather than *s,* is normal for the plural form of a word which is being quoted from something else, as in *There*

are too many <u>that's</u> in that sentence.

3. 's should be used to form the plural of single letters and figures, as in *Dot your i's and cross your t's*; *Write a row of 2's, then a row of 3's*. With longer numbers, e.g. in dates, both 's and s are permissible: *Were you around in the 1930's/1930s?*; *How many 30's/30s are there in 240?* An s alone should be used to form the plural of abbreviations made up of a sequence of initial letters: the correct plural of *M.P.*, for example, is *M.P.s,* not **M.P.'s.*

appendix

When the word **appendix** refers to an extra section of information placed at the end of a book, etc., the plural is usually **appendices,** but **appendixes** is also found and is correct. When **appendix** refers to a particular part of the intestine, **appendixes** is the correct plural form.

applicable

This word is nowadays increasingly often heard with the stress on the second syllable, but the pronunciation still preferred by the majority of English speakers has the stress on the first syllable. Neither pronunciation is wrong.

appreciate

In the sense of 'to be grateful', **appreciate** must be followed by an object: *I should appreciate it if you did that at once* is correct, **I should appreciate if you did that* is not.

apprehend see **comprehend.**

apt

When **apt** means 'having a tendency to', it is followed by **to,** as in *She is apt to say rather foolish things*. With the meaning, 'quick to learn, clever at, having an aptitude for', it may be followed by **at:** *Our new Treasurer has proved particularly apt at devising fund-raising projects.*
See also **liable.**

-ar see -er.

arbiter, arbitrator

The word **arbiter** is usually used to denote a person who has the power or influence to control or make decisions about something: *arbiters of fashion.*

An **arbitrator** is a person chosen by parties in a dispute to decide between them in order to settle the dispute. The word **arbiter** may quite correctly be used in this sense, but this is now very rare.

argument

Not ***arguement**.

around, round, about

In British English, **round** is generally used when a circular movement or direction is meant (as in *The earth moves round the sun; He ran round the corner; He lives round the corner; He was running round and round in circles*), and **around** when movement or situation within or over an area is intended (as in *I have travelled all around the world; The children were running around in the garden*). In the above examples with **round, around** would also be acceptable to many speakers of British English, especially in informal contexts, but **round** is far commoner. American English, on the other hand, prefers **around** to **round** in such contexts.

There are certain set phrases and idioms in which **round** and **around** are not interchangeable, such as *to shop around, all the year round, to have been around*. In cases of uncertainty, consult a dictionary.

Like **round, about** is more common in British English than American English. Like **around, about** in British English generally means 'within or over an area', as in *The children were running about in the garden; The cushions were scattered about the room*. In literary or formal English, **about** may also mean 'surrounding', as in *They built a wall about the city*.

About is also used in expressions of time, number, etc., as in *about four o'clock, about £20*. In informal speech and writing, **around** may be substituted for **about,** especially in expressions of time: *around four o'clock*.

artist, artiste

An **artist** is a person who paints pictures or one who is skilled in another of the fine arts such as sculpture or music: *a stained-glass artist*. In a more general sense, **artist** may be applied to anyone who shows great skill in what they do: *He is a real artist with a fishing-rod*.

An **artiste** (pronounced *är-tēst'*) is a performer in a theatre or circus, e.g. a singer, dancer, juggler, comedian, or, rather less frequently, an actor. The word **artist** may also be used in this sense.

as see **like.**

as ... as, so ... as

In making comparisons, one should use the form **as ... as,** as in

19

asphyxiate

He is as tall as his brother; I will come as soon as I can. After a negative word such as **not,** the first **as** may be replaced by **so:** both *It's not as difficult as you think* and *It's not so difficult as you think* are correct. When the second **as** is followed by **to** and an infinitive, the correct construction is **so . . . as:** *Do you think he would be so foolish as to come?*

asphyxiate

A word often misspelt. Note the *ph, y* and *x.*

assassinate

Another word which is commonly misspelt. Note that it has *ss* twice, but one *n.*

assent, consent

Both these verbs convey the notion of 'agreeing to' or 'complying with' something, but **consent** usually implies a much more positive or active decision than **assent.**

To **assent** to something (normally an opinion or proposal) is to agree with it, without any doubts, objections or persuasion: *He readily assented to their suggestions; They assented to the proposal to widen the road.* **Consent,** on the other hand, implies both that a certain amount of thought or persuasion has been involved in the decision-making process, and that the person consenting is giving in to or agreeing to comply with a request or proposal in spite of doubts or objections which he had and perhaps still has: *I felt he was too young to go into town alone, but in the end I consented; I will never consent to such a proposal.*

assume, presume

Assume, in the sense of 'to suppose, take as a fact', is very close in meaning to **presume.** Both these verbs mean 'to suppose (something) to be true without any definite proof', but **presume** implies a greater degree of certainty in one's belief than **assume,** which should be used when one is simply taking something as a basis for discussion or action. The difference between **assume** and **presume** can be seen in the following examples: *I presume John is coming because he told me yesterday he would be* (**presume** is correct here because there is a good basis for my belief); *I don't know whether John can come or not, but let's assume that he can and plan accordingly* (**assume** is appropriate here because John's coming is simply being proposed as a hypothesis on which to base plans.)

assurance, assure see insure.

as well see **also.**

-asy see **-acy.**

at see **in.**

aural see **oral.**

authoritarian, authoritative

Authoritarian means 'demanding obedience, considering obedience to authority more important than personal freedom': *authoritarian parents*; *an authoritarian government.*

Authoritative usually means 'having authority, said or done with authority', as in *an authoritative statement/opinion* (= one which can be relied on because the person making it has the necessary authority, status or expertise).

authority

When **authority** means 'an expert, a reliable source of information', it is usually followed by **on:** *He is an authority on Roman history.* When it means 'official power, power due to one's position or status', it is followed by **over:** *I have no authority over them.* When authority means 'right because of one's power, position, etc.', it is followed by **for** or by **to** and an infinitive: *You have no authority to question him*; *What authority do you have for questioning him?*

avenge, revenge, vengeance

The verbs **avenge** and **revenge** are almost identical in meaning, and indeed many people treat them as synonyms. However, these words do differ slightly in both meaning and use, and the differences are worth observing and preserving.

Revenge should be used when the subject of the verb is acting in retaliation for harm or suffering in order to satisfy his feelings of anger or resentment: *He vowed to revenge himself on his enemies for what they had done to him*; *He revenged the injustices he had suffered.* Usually the subject of the verb **revenge** is himself the person who suffered the offence.

Avenge is the correct verb to use when the subject of the verb is acting in retaliation for a wrong suffered (usually by someone else) in order to achieve justice of a sort by inflicting harm or suffering more or less equivalent to the original offence: *He vowed to avenge his father's death.*

The distinctions in meaning and use that exist between **avenge** and **revenge** similarly apply to the nouns **vengeance** and **revenge.**

averse see **adverse.**

await see **wait.**

awake, awaken see **wake.**

award, reward

An **award** is something given or received for excellence, merit or bravery: *He has received many awards for his dress designs.* **Award** also applies to something given or received as a result of a decision by a judge or arbitrator: *The accident victims each received an award of £2000.*

A **reward** is given or received in return for good work, a service rendered, etc., as in *A reward was offered for capturing the bandits; The children were very well-behaved, and were given 10p each as a reward.*

bachelor

This word is often incorrectly spelt *batchelor. Note that there is no *t* in the word.

bacillus see **bacterium.**

backward, backwards

As adverbs, both **backwards** and **backward** are correct: *She walked backwards out of the room; He fell over when he tried walking backward.* **Backwards** is commoner in British English and **backward** in American English.

As an adjective, only the form **backward** is correct: *a backward jump.* Note that when the adjective **backward** means 'towards the back', it always comes before the noun. When it means 'less advanced or less developed than is normal', it can precede or follow the noun: *a backward child; He is rather backward for his age.*

bacterium, bacillus, virus

The plural of **bacterium** is **bacteria. Bacteria** is sometimes used incorrectly as a singular noun; care should be taken to avoid this. The plurals of **bacillus** and **virus** are **bacilli** and **viruses** respectively.

Bacteria, bacilli and **viruses** may all be spoken of informally as *germs.* **Bacteria** are microscopic plants which can cause disease and putrefaction. **Bacillus** is correctly used to refer to any member of a particular group of rod-shaped bacteria, but the word is often loosely applied to any disease-causing bacterium. **Viruses** are much smaller than **bacteria,** and are complex substances, consisting of proteins, etc., which behave in some ways like living organisms. They can reproduce themselves only inside the living cells of plants or animal bodies, by doing which they usually cause disease.

bade see **bid.**

baggage

This word should only be used in the singular form, and with a singular verb, even when more than one piece of baggage is referred to: *My baggage consists of three suitcases.*
See also **luggage.**

bail, bale

Bail is money given to a court of law to gain the release of an untried prisoner until the time of his trial. To **bail out** a person is to get the person released from prison by providing bail.

To **bale out** means either 'to remove water from a boat' or 'to parachute from a plane in an emergency'. The spelling **bail out** is also possible with these meanings, but is much less common than **bale out.**

barbarian, barbaric, barbarous

A **barbarian** is a person belonging to a relatively uncivilized, but not primitive, society; used figuratively, it denotes a person whose behaviour is crude, rude or uncultured. The adjective **barbarian** means 'of, or typical of, barbarians': *barbarian tribes; barbarian splendour.*

Barbaric also means 'typical of barbarians'. It can be used of something one tolerates or even admires, or on the other hand of something one considers excessively or tastelessly showy: *barbaric simplicity; barbaric splendour.*

Barbarous means 'typical of, or as bad as, the worst or cruellest side of barbarian behaviour', and implies condemnation: *barbarous crimes.*

The above distinction between **barbaric** and **barbarous,** though backed by most authorities, is not always made by all speakers of English: **barbaric** is frequently used in the sense given here for **barbarous** and **barbarous** is occasionally seen or heard where **barbaric** would be more appropriate. In careful speech and writing, however, the distinction in meaning outlined here should be maintained.

bath, bathe

The verb to **bath** means 'to wash (usually the whole body) in a bath', as in *I'll bath the baby; She baths in cold water.* To **bathe** means 'to wash (a part of one's body) in order to make clean or lessen

23

pain', as in *He should bathe his feet in hot water*. In American English, **bathe** is used for both the **bath** and the **bathe** of British English. The verb **bathe** also means 'to go swimming', as in *The children went bathing in the sea every day.*

Note that the present participles and past tenses of **bath** and **bathe** are identical in writing: **bathing** and **bathed.**

beast see **animal.**

beautiful, beauty

Care should be taken with the spelling of these words. Note the *eau.*

because

Because should not be used to introduce a subordinate clause referring back to **reason** or **reason why** in a main clause (as in **The reason (why) he stole the money is because he wanted to buy food*), since the **because** in such a construction simply duplicates the information already conveyed by **reason** or **reason why.** The correct construction is with **that,** not **because,** as in *The reason (why) he stole the money is that he wanted to buy food.*

because of, due to, owing to

Because of and **owing to** are used to introduce adverbial phrases explaining the reason for something described by the <u>verb</u> of the sentence, as in *The match was cancelled because of the heavy rain* and *Owing to the bad weather, half the guests didn't come.* **Due to** is often also used in this way (as in *The match was cancelled due to the heavy rain*), but many people consider this to be incorrect, and the use of **due to** in such constructions should be avoided in careful speech and writing, although it is now quite acceptable and very common in informal speech. In careful, formal English, **due** should always be treated as an adjective and **due to** must therefore follow or refer back to a <u>noun</u>: compare *His success was due to hard work* and *The cancellation of the match was due to the heavy rain* with *The match was cancelled because of the rain.*

begin, commence, start

The verb **begin** is more usual and less formal than **commence** but slightly less informal than the verb **start.** **Begin** and **start** may be followed by either **to** and an infinitive or a verb ending in **-ing:** *He began to read* or *He began reading; He started to sing* or *He started singing.* **Commence** is always followed by a verb ending in **-ing:** *He commenced reading.*

below, beneath, under, underneath

It is not easy to give a clear and concise description of the different meanings and uses of these four words, and all that is attempted here is to provide a few guidelines.

Underneath is mostly used when two things are touching or very close to each other, often with the implication of one thing covering the other: *He lifted the stone to see what was underneath it*; *Underneath, he found a piece of paper*; *The key is underneath the mat*. Even where the two things linked by **underneath** are not so close together, there is often still an implication of the one thing completely covering or sheltering the other: *The mouse hid underneath the chair*. **Underneath** is also used to refer to people's 'hidden qualities', as in *He seems uncaring but he's a kind man underneath*.

The word **under** is used when there is a fairly close or direct connection between the things being referred to, especially where one thing is on or directly above the other: *He could feel the branch shaking under him* (i.e. he was sitting or lying on it); *The mouse ran under the chair*; *The river flows under a bridge at that point*. **Below** on the other hand means 'at or to a lower level than', and the relationship between the things referred to is usually less close or direct: *He could see cows and sheep in the valley below him* (i.e. he is looking down from a hill; the valley is not literally under his feet).

Under and **below** are both used also in a figurative sense, and here again there is a more direct relationship between things related by **under** than between things related by **below**: compare, for example, *He has twenty people under him* (= he is in charge of, has authority over, twenty people) and *There are twenty people below him* (= there are twenty people lower in rank than him, or in less important positions than his; he may not, however, have authority over any of them).

Beneath is felt by many people to be more formal, archaic or literary than **below** or **under** when used to describe the position of one thing in relationship to another. However, in certain figurative uses, **beneath** must be used: *His behaviour was beneath contempt*; *He thought it beneath him to clean the house*.

benign, benignant, malign, malignant

In medical contexts, **benign** means 'not fatal or harmful to health', as in *a benign tumour*. The opposite of **benign** in this sense is **malignant**: *a malignant growth*.

In other contexts, **benign** and **malign** should generally be used when it is the impact, influence or effect of a person, action or thing that is being referred to, and **benignant** and **malignant** when it is intentions, attitudes, feelings or personalities that are being spoken of: *a benign/malign influence* but *He is benignant/malignant by nature*. However, these distinctions are by no means consistently observed by all English-speakers: in particular, **benign** is frequently used in the sense given here for **benignant,** as in *a benign smile,* and this use is so well established that is must now be accepted as correct.

beside, besides

The preposition **beside** means 'next to, at the side of', as in *He was standing beside me.* **Besides** means 'as well as, in addition to, except', as in *Is anyone coming besides John?*

Besides may also function as an adverb, meaning 'as well, moreover': *These shoes are very expensive, and besides, they're too small*; *She has three sons and an adopted daughter besides.*

between, among

It is frequently stated by purists that since **between** is derived from the same root as the word *two*, it must only be used to link two nouns or pronouns, and that where there are three or more nouns or pronouns to be related in a sentence, **among** rather than **between** must be used. This is by no means the case. Where there is a sense of sharing out or dividing up, it is certainly desirable to use **between** for two people or things and **among** for larger numbers: *The sweets were shared between the two children*; *The sweets were shared out among all the children in the class.* But where the sentence is referring to agreements, relationships, position, etc., **between** is quite correctly used to relate three or more things, as in *Switzerland is situated between France, Germany, Austria and Italy* or *discussions between shareholders, employers and trade unionists.* (Note that in this last example, **between** conveys the notion that all three groups are involved in the same discussion, whereas **among** would suggest that each group is holding a separate discussion.)

The second or last of the words being related by **between** should correctly be preceded by **and,** not *or.* Although an expression like *a choice between whisky or brandy* is perhaps acceptable in informal speech, it should be avoided in formal contexts: *between whisky and brandy* is the correct construction.

Between should not be followed by a singular noun on its own, since by virtue of its meaning it must relate two or more things. It is therefore incorrect to say, for example, *He paused between each sentence.* Say, rather, *He paused between sentences* or *He paused after each* *sentence.*

For the incorrect use of **I** after **between,** see **me.**

biannual see **biennial.**

bid

When **bid** means 'to make an offer, make a bid', the past tense and past participle are **bid:** *John bid £500 for the painting.* In the archaic, literary or formal sense of 'to ask, say or tell', the past tense is usually **bade,** the past participle usually **bidden,** as in *He bade me enter, He bade me farewell,* but **bid** is sometimes used as the past tense and past participle of the verb in this sense also.

Bade is generally pronounced [*bad*], but [*bād*] is also permitted, especially in poetry.

biennial, biannual

Biennial means 'happening, etc. every two years', **biannual** 'happening, etc. twice a year'. When applied to plants, **biennial** means '(a plant) that lives for two years'.

See also **bi-weekly,** etc.

big, great, large

In general, **big** and **large** refer to size, **great** to importance, quality, etc., but the distinctions are not always as clear-cut as this rule might suggest. In referring to size, **big** means 'not small', 'not as small as most others of the same type': *a big dog; a big book; He is big for his age* (= bigger than most people of his age). **Big** may also refer to age: *When I'm big, I'm going to be a policeman* (= when I'm grown up, an adult). **Big** has the meaning 'important, powerful' in constructions like *He is a big man in banking; This is a big day for us.*

Large is more formal than **big,** and always refers to size or amount: *a large dog; a large book; A large crowd gathered; A large number of people were there.* (Note that one can say *a big crowd* but not *a big number of people* — **big** cannot be used when referring to numbers, only sizes.)

Great is mostly used to refer to quality rather than size: *He is a great man; a great writer; This is a great day for us; You have been a really great audience; We're great friends* (= very friendly). When used to refer to size or extent, it usually means 'exceptionally large, long, etc.', 'large and impressive': *He lived to a great age; The cathedral is entered through a great doorway in the west wall.* **Great** may also be used to lend emphasis to other words: *a great many people; a great big dog.*

billion see **million.**

bi-weekly, bimonthly, *etc.*

Notice that these words are ambiguous, meaning that something happens, etc. 'twice a week, month, etc.' or 'once every two weeks, months, etc.'. If the context does not make your meaning clear, serious confusion could arise: in such cases, these terms should be replaced by unambiguous words such as **two-monthly, fortnightly, half-yearly, twice-weekly,** etc.

blatant see **flagrant.**

blond, blonde

Blond is masculine, **blonde** feminine: *He is blond*; *She is blonde*; *She is a blonde*; *She has blonde hair*; *He has blond hair*. Some authorities would allow *She has blond hair* since here the **blond** refers not to *she* but *hair*, but *She has blonde hair* is commoner.

born, borne

Borne is the usual past participle of the verb **to bear,** both in the senses of 'to carry' and 'to give birth to': *He was borne shoulder-high after his victory*; *She has borne him seven children*.

Born may only be used, and must be used, in passive constructions when the verb is not followed by the preposition **by:** *She was born in London*; *She was born of Indian parents*; but *She was borne by an Indian girl*.

both

Both should be followed by **and,** not *as well as: *He is both rich as well as handsome* is incorrect; the correct form of the sentence would be *He is both rich and handsome*.

Care must be taken to place **both** and **and** correctly in a sentence, so that what follows the **and** is all and only that which is being linked or related to what follows **both:** for example, *She has succeeded both as a journalist and a publisher* is not correct; either the *as* should precede the *both*, so that what is being related is *a journalist* and *a publisher*, or there should be an *as* after the *both* and the *and* so that what is being linked is *as a journalist* and *as a publisher*.

brethren see **brothers.**

broad, wide

The adjectives **broad** and **wide** can often be used interchangeably to describe a noun: *a wide road/river* is essentially the same as *a broad road/river*. However, these two words are not absolutely synonymous and in some contexts only the one or the other is appropriate.

The difference between **broad** and **wide** is that **broad** refers to the extent across something, whereas **wide** refers to the distance separating, or gap between, its sides or edges. Hence one speaks, for example, of a person's _broad back_ but a jacket's _wide sleeves_.

brothers, brethren

The normal plural of **brother** is **brothers. Brethren** is an archaic plural, but is still used for the members of certain organizations, especially religious orders.

bus

The plural of **bus** is **buses,** not ***busses.**

can, may

In careful speech and writing, **may** should be used when the idea of 'giving permission, allowing something' is intended: _You may go to the party if you wish_ (= I am giving you permission to go). **Can** should only be used to convey the idea of 'ability, possibility': _I can speak Chinese; You can walk to the party if you miss the bus._ However, in informal speech **can** is frequently used instead of **may**: _You can go to the party if you want to._

can not, cannot

In British English, the form **cannot** must be used unless the word **not** is linked to the following word or words in a way that requires it to have particular emphasis. Compare for example _He cannot sing_ and _You cannot just walk into the room without knocking on the door first_ with _He can not only sing but he dances as well._ In American English, **can not** may be used, and is generally preferred, where British English requires **cannot**.

In informal speech and writing, **cannot** is usually replaced by the shortened form **can't**.

capital letters

Capital letters must be used at the beginning of every sentence. Capitals are also required for the first letter of the names of people, countries, etc., and of words derived from them: _John_; _Anne_; _Sir Bernard Smith_; _Australia_; _the Australian cricket team_; _South Africa_; _a South African plant_; _Christ_; _Christian_; _Marx_; _Marxist_; _Chestnut Avenue._ Similarly, capitals must be used for the first letter of all important words in the titles of books, plays, people, organizations, and so on: _the Bay of Bengal_; _the Prince of Wales_; _Admiral of the Fleet Lord Brown_; _Department of Health and Social Services_; _a book_ entitled 'The Biggest Fish in the World'. (Note that the first word of a book's or play's title must always have a capital letter also.) When a title is hyphenated, both parts have a capital letter: *Major-General Smith*.

Words which require a capital in names and titles do not of course need one in other circumstances: *the Republic of South Africa* but *South Africa is a republic*; *the President of the United States* (= a particular person) but *How many presidents of the United States have there been?*; *South America* but *the south of England*.

A few minor points are worth noting:

1. Seasons should not normally have capitals, but it may occasionally be necessary to write *Spring* rather than *spring* for the sake of clarity.

2. Many words which are in origin proper names or derived from proper names do not take a capital: *pasteurize, wellington, sandwich, watt, ampere*. In some cases, forms with and without capitals are equally correct: *plaster of paris/Paris*; *platonic/Platonic love*. If you are uncertain, consult a dictionary.

3. *Sir, madam*, etc. should always have a capital at the beginning of a letter: *Dear Sir*.

care

The verb **care** may be followed by the prepositions **for, about** or **to.**

Care for means 'to look after, take care of (someone)', as in *Nurses care for their patients*. **Care for** also means 'to like', as in *I don't care for flowers very much*.

When **care** means 'to be concerned or worried', it is often followed by **about**: *She doesn't care about what other people think*. Sometimes **care** may be used on its own in this sense: *I don't care what you do*.

Care to is a rather formal expression meaning 'to like to, wish to', as in *Would you care to have dinner with me this evening?*

cattle

Cattle is a plural noun, and must therefore be followed by a plural, not a singular, verb: *The cattle were taken to market*.

-ce, -cy nouns

Most words ending in **-ent** or **-ant,** and many other words, have related nouns ending in **-ce** or **-cy.** In the majority of cases, only the one form or the other is normal or correct:

agent	:	agency	avoid	:	avoidance
decent	:	decency	intelligent	:	intelligence
vacant	:	vacancy	magnificent	:	magnificence

In general, longer words tend to end in **-ce,** shorter ones in **-cy.**

In some cases, both forms are permissible:

| consistent | : | consistence, consistency |
| irrelevant | : | irrelevance, irrelevancy |

In certain of these cases, there is a clear difference in meaning between the **-ce** noun and the **-cy** noun: compare *dependence* (= the condition of being dependent) and *dependency* (= a territory dependent on another country), *emergence* and *emergency,* *excellence* and *excellency* (as in *His Excellency the Ambassador*).

In other cases, there may be little or no discernible difference in meaning between the two forms, e.g. *complacence, complacency,* but one form may be commoner than the other, e.g. *competence* and the rarer form *competency.* In the case of *consistence/consistency,* the latter must be used when 'the state of being consistent' is meant, but either form is acceptable in the sense of 'degree of thickness of a liquid'.

-ce, -se, *etc.* in British and American English

Should one write *defence* or *defense, practice* or *practise*? If *offence* is correct, is the related adjective spelt *offencive* or *offensive*? In what ways does American usage differ from British usage?

There are, unfortunately, few general rules to help the writer through this orthographic minefield, but the following points are worth noting:

1.   Words which are pronounced with a *z*-sound are written with an *s*: *advise, devise, exercise, expertise, revise, treatise,* etc. (See also the article **-ise, -ize**).

2.   Words which are pronounced with an *s*-sound immediately following a vowel are generally written with a *c*: *advice, deduce, device, justice, lice, mice, office, rejoice, voice,* etc. Among the exceptions to this rule are *house, louse, mouse, obtuse, profuse, promise.* Note in particular the spelling of *prophecy* and the related verb *prophesy.*

3.   Words which are related to words ending in **-ant** and **-ent** are written with a *c*: *difference, ignorance, impudence,* etc. (see **-ce, -cy nouns** for further examples).

Words which are pronounced with an *s*-sound following a consonant may have either *c* or *s* in writing:

Among the words written with *c* are *advance, commence, com-*

merce, dance, fence, finance, hence, pence, pronounce, reverence, romance, and *since*. Among the words written with an *s* are *dense, endorse, immense, recompense, response, sense* and *tense*.

For the difference between *counsel* and *council*, see **counsel, council**.

The above rules apply in both British and American English. However, there are a number of words in which these two forms of English differ in usage:

In British English, *licence* and *practice* are nouns, *license* and *practise* the related verbs. In American English, the forms *license* and *practice* are used for both noun and verb.

In British English, the nouns *defence, offence* and *pretence* are spelt with a *c*, but in American English they are written with an *s*. Note that the related adjectives *defensive* and *offensive* are written with an *s* in both British and American English.

The noun *vice* (= a fault or bad habit) is written with *c* in both American and British English, but *vice* (= a tool with metal jaws for holding things firmly) is written with *c* in British English and *s* in American English.

-cede, -ceed, -sede

Most words ending in [-*sēd*] are spelt **-cede**. Three words which end in **-ceed** are *exceed, proceed*, and *succeed*. Only *supersede* ends in **-sede**.

censor, censure

A **censor** is an official who examines books, films, letters, etc. and who has the power to delete parts of the material or to forbid publication, showing, etc. **Censure** is criticism or blame.

centre, middle

Although these two words are sometimes thought of as synonyms, there are slight differences between them in meaning and use. Firstly, **centre** has a connotation of exactness lacking in **middle:** the *centre* of a room is at (or at least very close to) a point equally far from the walls of the room, whereas the *middle* of the room covers a much larger and more vaguely defined area. In referring to long things, **middle** rather than **centre** is normal: *the middle of the road*.

In a figurative sense, **centre** implies a degree of influence or agency, **middle** only involvement: *He is the centre of a dispute* means the dispute is over him or something he has or has not done; *He is in the middle of a dispute* means only that he is involved in it, whatever its cause.

The phrase **centre round/around** is frequently condemned, but must now be considered correct in informal speech. In formal contexts, however, it is perhaps better to avoid this construction, and use **centre on** or **be centred in/on** instead.

ceremonial, ceremonious

The adjective **ceremonial** means 'pertaining to or appropriate for a formal ceremony', as *ceremonial dress*; *a ceremonial occasion*. **Ceremonial** may also be used as a noun, meaning 'a ceremony, rite' or 'ceremonial rules or ritual'.

Ceremonious is most often applied to a person or his behaviour and means 'much concerned with ceremony, carefully formal or polite', usually with the implication of being excessively or inappropriately so.

chance

As a verb, **chance** may be followed by **on** before a noun, as in *I chanced on a friend of yours in the library* (= I met him by accident), or by **to** plus a verb, as in *I chanced to meet him in the library.*

The noun **chance** may be followed by **of, on,** or **to.** With the meaning 'possibility', **chance** is correctly followed by **of:** *There's no chance of success/succeeding.* Followed by **to, chance** means 'opportunity': *I want a chance to meet the President too.* In the phrase **take a chance** 'to gamble, take a risk', chance is followed by **on,** as in *She took a chance on the train's being late in leaving.*

charge

In charge of means 'in control of, responsible for', as in *The policeman asked who had been in charge of the dog.*

In the charge of means 'in the care of, being looked after by', as in *The children were in the charge of two teachers.*

childish, childlike

Childish and **childlike** both mean 'of or like a child', but in a bad and a good sense respectively: a person may be liked for his *childlike innocence,* but will be disliked if he makes *childish remarks* or indulges in *childish tantrums.*

chord see cord.

chronic

The use of the adjective **chronic** in the sense of 'very bad, deplorable' is slang, or at best informal. It should be avoided in formal speech and writing.

circumstances

Both **in the circumstances** and **under the circumstances** are acceptable.

clad see **clothed.**

clandestine

As yet, the only accepted pronunciation for this word is [*klan-des'tin*]. Both [*klan-des'tīn*] and [*klan'des-tīn*] are common, but neither of these has yet met with the general approval of the authorities.

classic, classical

A **classic** is 'an established work of art or literature of high quality': *Dickens' novels are considered classics.* The plural **classics** is used to denote 'Greek and Latin studies', as in *He is studying classics at university.*

The adjective pertaining to the noun **classic** in the above sense is also **classic:** *Dickens' novels are among the classic works of English literature.* However, the adjective denoting 'pertaining to the classics (= Greek and Latin studies), or to Greece and Rome' is **classical:** *classical studies; a classical education; classical writers.*

Classic also means 'typical' (as in *a classic example of his stupidity; the classic symptoms of this disease*) and 'simple or balanced in form' (as in *classic clothes; a building of classic proportions*).

Classical, as applied to music, means 'traditional in form, following the style of the great composers of the past'.

clean, cleanse

To **clean** something is to 'remove dirt, etc. from' it: *I must clean the car/toilet this morning.* The verb **cleanse** (pronounced [*klenz*]) may also be used to mean 'to remove dirt, germs, etc. from' something, especially a part of the body, as in *This cream will cleanse the skin* or *She cleansed the wound,* but is more often used figuratively to mean 'to make pure, free from wickedness', as in *He asked God to cleanse him of his sins.*

A **cleanser** is a substance which cleans or cleanses, for example a cosmetic for cleaning the skin when removing make-up or a soap or detergent used for cleaning sinks, etc.

Note that in many parts of Britain at least, it is the local authority's *Cleansing* Department which is responsible for cleaning the streets and removing household refuse.

client, clientele see **customer.**

clothed, clad

The current normal past tense and past participle of **clothe** is **clothed.** The form **clad** is archaic, but is still used in some compounds and phrases, such as *lightly clad, armour-clad, ironclad,* and when referring to specific types of clothing, as in *knights clad in armour* or *fishermen clad in oilskins.* **Clad** may of course be substituted for **clothed** in any context in which one wishes to use an archaic form for literary or facetious reasons.

In figurative and poetic contexts, both **clad** and **clothed** are possible, but **clothed** is now more common: *a hillside clothed in yellow flowers.*

coarse, course

Note the spelling of these two words. **Coarse** is an adjective meaning 'rude, crude, rough'. **Course** is the correct spelling for the noun meaning 'series, route, etc.', and for the rather literary verb meaning 'to run': *We're off course*; *Tears coursed down her cheeks*; *Of course, I knew that already.*

coherence, cohesion

Both these words mean 'sticking together'. **Coherence** refers to the degree to which a person's thoughts, statements, etc. 'join together' logically, intelligibly or consistently. **Cohesion** refers to the literal sticking together of two things, or in a figurative sense, of people in a group, etc.: *the cohesion of the family unit.*

collective nouns

Collective nouns are singular nouns referring to groups of people, animals, things, etc. There is often some uncertainty as to whether such nouns should be followed by a singular or a plural verb. In attempting to resolve this difficulty, we shall find that collective nouns can be divided into two main categories, and we shall deal with each in turn.

    1.   One type of collective noun is that which denotes a number of articles collected together as a group or considered as a class e.g. *furniture, luggage, baggage, cutlery.* Such nouns are always used in the singular and must be followed by a singular verb: *Your luggage is in the luggage-rack above you.*

    2.   The second main category of collective nouns comprises nouns (mostly referring to people) which in the singular denote a group which may be thought of either as a number of separate individuals or as a single unit. With such nouns, the following verb should be plural when the group is regarded as comprising separate individuals, singular when regarded as a

unit: *The committee meets every Tuesday; The committee were unable to make up their minds; The orchestra was/were playing well.* Among the nouns in this category are:

audience	crew	group
class	crowd	jury
club	family	orchestra
committee	firm	public
company	government	team

Note that not only verbs but also pronouns relating to these nouns may be singular or plural, and one must be particularly careful to make verbs and pronouns consistent in this respect: *The audience are asked to remain in their seats* is correct, **The audience is asked to remain in their seats* is not.

Unlike the nouns of the first category, most of the nouns in this group can also be used in the plural, e.g. *committees, clubs, orchestras,* and so on, followed of course by plural verbs and pronouns.

There are a number of other words which pose problems of verb-agreement similar to those of the second category of collective nouns just dealt with. Among these are *rest* and *number*. When a noun phrase including *rest* refers to a unit or an amount, it is followed by a singular verb, as in *The west wall has crumbled but the rest of the castle is still standing,* whereas if it refers to a group, it is followed by a plural verb, as in *Three people in the bus died in the accident. The rest of the passengers were fortunate to receive only minor injuries.* (This rule of singular/plural agreement applies equally to phrases including fractions, *most, some,* etc., e.g. *Most of the passengers were hurt; Most of the castle is still standing.*)

A noun phrase consisting of *a number of* followed by a plural noun is correctly followed by a plural verb: *A number of children were playing in the street.* In this construction, *a number of* is treated as an adjective phrase, and the verb is made to agree with the plural noun it follows. This use of *number* must be distinguished from the very similar construction *the number of* followed by a plural noun, which is followed by a singular verb agreeing with the singular noun *number: The number of children in the town is rising.*

See also the article **group terms** for the correct use of *flock, herd, shoal,* etc.

colon

A colon is correctly used in a sentence when the statement that follows the colon explains, balances, or completes in some way the statement that precedes it, as in *I have something to tell you: John is coming tomorrow*; *This is an excellent play: the characters are believable, the action gripping, and the ending unexpected*; *There is just one thing I would like: a new car.*

A colon is also used to mark the beginning of a list of items as in *We need the following things: string, paper, glue, scissors, and a pencil.* Sometimes the colon preceding a list is followed by a dash (:–), especially if the list begins on a new line, but although not incorrect, this is quite unnecessary, and the dash is in general best omitted.

A third use of the colon is to introduce quoted speech, as in *John suddenly shouted: 'Look out! He's coming back!'*; a comma is also correctly used for this purpose, especially in recording casual conversation.

combat

The verb **combat** means 'to fight against', and should therefore not be followed by the preposition **against:** **He combated against the government's plans to build a motorway* is incorrect. **Combated** on its own is sufficient and correct: *He combated the plans.* This use of **combat** is rather formal.

comic, comical

The adjective **comic** means 'pertaining to comedy', 'intended to amuse', as in *a comic actor*; *comic opera*. **Comical** means 'funny, amusing', and applies to anything which causes laughter whether intended to do so or not: *a comical sight*. **Comic** is increasingly often used in this sense also, but **comical** may not be used in the sense given for **comic** above.

comma

In general, a comma marks a pause or slight break in a sentence, a less complete separation than one indicated by a semi-colon, a full stop, or brackets. The rules governing the use of the comma may seem complicated, but the complexity is more apparent than real. In certain situations a comma is obligatory; in others a comma is optional and its use is a matter of individual taste or a means of avoiding ambiguities and awkward or unclear constructions. Commas should be used sparingly: if a sentence you have written contains or seems to require a lot of commas, then the sentence is probably too long or too complex to be easily understood, and should be rewritten.

Commas are generally inserted between two or more adjectives preceding a noun: *a big, red car*; *a cold, wet, windy day*. There are, however, a number of exceptions to this rule:

1. When two adjectives together convey a single idea, they should not be separated by a comma: for example, in *a great big dog*, *great* modifies *big* and serves to emphasize the bigness of the dog; similarly in *Good old Sam!*, *good* and *old* together form a single expression denoting approval or praise, and should therefore not be separated by a comma.

2. If the last adjective is more closely linked to the following noun than the other adjective(s) or if it forms a single unit with the following noun, then it should not be preceded by a comma: *a foolish old man* (= an old man who is foolish); *a pretty little girl* (= a little girl who is pretty); *a bigger/different green pen* (= a green pen which is bigger than or different from some other green pen).

It follows from what has been said here that a comma may be appropriate in one sentence but wrong in an otherwise identical sentence, depending on the meaning to be conveyed. For example, *He bought a new, red car* means that he bought a new car which happened to be red, whereas *He bought a new red car* (with no comma) means that he already had a red car which he replaced with another red car.

(A useful test which may help you to decide whether or not to insert a comma between two adjectives is to substitute an *and* for the proposed comma: if you can put an *and* in, then put in a comma; if you can't, don't. One could not, for example, say **a great and big dog* or **Good and old Sam!*, but one could say *a cold and wet and windy day*.)

3. When two or more adjectives are linked by *and*, no comma should be inserted: *a great and wise king*; *Our king is great and wise and just*. However, if the *and* links the last two adjectives in a series of adjectives otherwise separated only by commas, it also may correctly be preceded by a comma: both *a great, wise and just king* and *a great, wise, and just king* are correct. (Whichever style one chooses, one should at least try to be consistent, however.) Of course, if the last two adjectives together form a unit, a comma should not be inserted: *a big, yellow and green bus* is correct, **a big, yellow, and green bus* is not.

Essentially the same rules as have been given above for series of adjectives apply to the insertion or omission of commas between nouns, verbs, phrases, and clauses, as can be seen from the following examples: *He washed the cups, saucers(,) and plates* (the comma between *saucers* and *and* could be omitted); *I like swim-*

ming, tennis(*,*) *and football*; *She sings and dances*; *She sings, dances*(*,*) *and paints*; *She took out her keys, opened the door*(*,*) *and went in* (the longer the phrases or clauses linked, the more likely the optional comma is to be inserted).

When there is a balance or contrast between clauses linked by a conjunction, they are usually separated by a comma, but if there is a close connection between the clauses, there should be no comma: *She's a pretty girl, but not very clever*; *Do that again and I'll smack you!* If there is no conjunction between the clauses, a comma is usually inserted, as in *When he arrived, the children hugged him* (compare *The children hugged him when he arrived* without a comma).

Introductory words, words which form a parenthesis, or the name of the person being spoken to, should be separated from the rest of the sentence by commas: *I don't like the idea. However, you may do as you please*; *John, I'm pleased to say, did not take part in the prank*; *You, Mary, must come back tomorrow.* Notice in particular the difference between *The boy who was wearing a cap laughed* and *The boy, who was wearing a cap, laughed*: in the first sentence, the clause *who was wearing a cap* is closely linked to *boy* and serves to identify the boy concerned, whereas in the second sentence, the same clause is simply given as an additional piece of information.

A comma may be used, like a colon, before direct speech: *Peter said, 'I want to come too'*. And a comma is normally placed after *Dear Sir*, etc. at the beginning of a handwritten letter and after *Yours sincerely*, etc. at the end of the letter, but is frequently omitted in a typewritten letter.

A comma is not needed between the month and year in dates, nor between the number and the street name in addresses.

Especial care should be taken not to separate subjects from verbs or verbs from their objects by inserting a comma between them. This is often done in an attempt to clarify the structure of a sentence, e.g. when the subject is a long and complex clause, but is not correct: for example, the comma between *killed* and *ate* in **The mouse that John's little black and white cat killed, ate the cheese* should be omitted as it divides the verb *ate* from the subject of the verb. If a sentence is so complicated as to appear to require a comma in such a position for the sake of clarity, the sentence should be rewritten.

commemorate

A word often misspelt. Note that the *e* is preceded by two *m*'s but followed by only one.

commence see **begin.**

commitment, committal

The normal noun meaning 'the act of committing' or 'the state of being committed' is **commitment**: *his commitment to our cause*; *I have a number of family commitments*; *commitment of the facts to paper*; *the commitment of a crime*. **Commital** is a rather formal or technical word which is normally used for the act of committing a person to prison or to a mental hospital or a body to the grave. It is also sometimes used for the act of committing a crime.

Note that **commitment** has a single *t* before the suffix, **committal** a double *t*.

committee

This is a word which is frequently misspelt. Note that it has two *m*'s and two *t*'s.

See also **collective nouns.**

common, mutual

Common means 'belonging to, or shared by, two or more people, etc.', as in *We share a common language*; *our common love of classical music*; *This knowledge is common to all of us.*

Mutual, strictly speaking, means 'given by each to the other or others involved and received by each from the other or others involved', and implies a two-way flow of feelings, etc., as in *their mutual respect* and *Their dislike was mutual.* Some people disapprove of the use of **mutual** in the sense of 'common' given above, as in *our mutual friend/acquaintance* or *a matter of mutual interest*, but this use is well-established and there is no reason to avoid it in phrases such as these, at least in informal speech and writing. In formal English it is better to keep to the distinction in meaning outlined above and speak of, for example, *a matter of common interest*, but *a mutual friend* and *mutual acquaintance* are now virtually set phrases acceptable in any style of speech.

Care should be taken not to use the word **mutual** superfluously in a sentence in which the notion of 'two-wayness' is already conveyed by some other word or words. For example, **their mutual respect for each other* is incorrect, as *mutual* and *for each other* convey the same information; one should say either *their mutual respect* or *their respect for each other*. Similarly, **We have come to a mutual agreement* is incorrect, as *agreement* itself means that both parties are involved and **mutual** is therefore superfluous.

comparable, comparative

Comparable means 'of the same kind, on the same scale, to the same degree, etc.': *The houses were comparable in size.* **Comparative** means 'judged by comparing with something else': *When the children stopped playing express trains, we had comparative quiet* (i.e. it may not have been absolutely quiet, but it was quieter than it had been before).

Care must be taken not to use **comparative** or the adverb **comparatively** in contexts where there is no explicit or implicit comparison being made. **Comparatively** in particular is frequently used where **fairly**, **rather**, or **quite** would be more appropriate. See also the next article.

compare, comparable, comparison

Compare should be followed by the preposition **to** when it means 'to point out or suggest similarities between things that are essentially different', as in *She compared him to a monkey*; *He compared his girlfriend to a rose.* When **compare** means 'to examine in order to find similarities, differences, relative merits, etc.', it should be followed by the preposition **with**: *If you compare this book with that one, you will find this one far better.*

Like **compare**, the adjective **comparable** may be followed by **to** or **with** depending on the sense in which it is used.

In set phrases with **compared** or **as compared**, both **with** and **to** are correct, but the meaning is always that of **compare with**: *Compared to/with you I'm an absolute genius*; *His house is a palace as compared to/with mine.*

The phrase **by/in comparison** must be followed by **with**, not **to**, as the sense is always that of **compare with** given above: *This book may seem expensive, but it is cheap in comparison with some you see in the shops.* **Comparison** should of course be followed by **to** when the sense is that of **compare to** given above: *I thought his comparison of the managing director to an ignorant baboon was quite uncalled-for.*

comparison of adjectives and adverbs

I Comparison of adjectives

Adjectives are describing words, such as *tall*, *beautiful*. It is possible for a person or thing to have more or less of the quality described by an adjective than another person or thing, and when we compare people or things with regard to some quality or another, we often use comparative forms of adjectives (such as *taller*, *more beautiful*) or superlative forms (*tallest*, *most beautiful*). Comparative adjectives should be used when two people or things are being compared, as in *John is older than Mary.* Superlatives should be used when three or more things are being compared: *All four boys are tall, but Peter is the tallest.* This rule is broken in a few set phrases, such as *may the best man win* or *put your best foot forward*, but should be adhered to in all other cases.

As can be seen above, there are two ways of treating the original adjective, either by adding **-er** and **-est** to it or by putting **more** or **most** in front of it. Adjectives of one syllable take **-er/-est**: *old, older, oldest*; *hard, harder, hardest*. Two-syllable adjectives which end in *-y*, *-ow*, *-le* and *-er* also take the **-er/-est** endings: *silly, sillier, silliest*; *narrow, narrower, narrowest*; *simple, simpler, simplest*; *clever, cleverer, cleverest*. A number of other two-syllable adjectives also take these endings, among the commonest of which are *common, quiet, polite, wicked, stupid, pleasant, civil*, and *handsome*. Some of these may equally form comparatives and superlatives with **more** and **most**, e.g. *polite*.

Other two-syllable adjectives and most longer adjectives take **more** and **most**: *tiring, more tiring, most tiring*; *beautiful, more beautiful, most beautiful*. One important exception to this is three-syllable negative adjectives formed from two-syllable adjectives which take the **-er/-est** endings; these also take **-er** and **-est**, e.g. *unhappy, unhappier, unhappiest*.

There are certain important spelling rules which must be observed in the formation of comparatives and superlatives:

1. When the adjective ends in *e*, the *e* is dropped before **-er** and **-est** are added: *white, whiter, whitest*. If the adjective ends in two *e*'s, one *e* is dropped: *free, freer, freest*.

2. If the adjective ends in a single consonant, if the vowel preceding that consonant is written with a single letter, and if the vowel and consonant are part of a stressed syllable, the consonant is doubled before **-er** and **-est**: *red, redder, reddest*; *big, bigger, biggest*; but great, greater, greatest (not *greatter*, because the vowel is written with two letters); *stupid, stupider, stupidest* (not *stupidder*, because the stress is on the first syllable). Note, however, that a final *l* is doubled in any case: *cruel, crueller, cruellest*.

3. A final *y* changes to *i* before **-er** and **-est**: *funny, funnier, funniest*. However, in the case of certain one-syllable words, both *y* and *i* are permitted: *shy, shyer or shier, shyest or shiest*; similarly *slyer, slyest or slier, sliest* and *wryer, wryest or wrier, wriest*. In the case of *dry, drier* and *driest* are the preferred forms; in the case of *spry, spryer* and *spryest* are preferred.

II Comparison of adverbs

Comparative and superlative forms of adverbs are formed in the same way as those of adjectives: adverbs ending in -*ly* take **more** and **most**, most others add **-er** and **-est** (e.g. *fast, faster, fastest*).

compel, impel

Compel means 'to force', as in *I was compelled to resign; They compelled me to betray my country.* **Impel** means 'to urge or drive (someone to do something)', as in *Hunger impelled the boy to steal.*

Compel should be used when there is a sense of irresistible force or pressure exerted on a person by some other person or thing, **impel** when the person is being driven to some action by his or her own feelings, needs, etc.

complement, compliment, supplement

A **complement** is 'that which, with some other thing, makes something which is complete or perfect' as in *Good wine is a complement to good food; Intuition is a complement to reason.* A ship's *complement* is the full number of officers and crew that the ship has or ought to have. A **compliment** is 'an expression of praise or flattery' as in *He is always paying me compliments.* The same distinction applies to the verbs **complement** and **compliment**: *Good wine complements good food; He complimented her on her work.*

The difference between **complement** and **supplement** is that a **complement** makes something complete, while a **supplement** is something added to something else which is already complete, e.g. as a bonus or to make up for some deficiency in it: *a newspaper's colour supplement.* This distinction equally applies to the verbs **complement** and **supplement**: *She supplements her diet with vitamin pills.*

compose see comprise.

comprehend, apprehend

Among their various meanings, both **comprehend** and **apprehend** may be used in the sense of 'to understand'. They are not, however, synonymous.

To **comprehend** is 'to understand something completely, to understand the reasons for (something)'. To **apprehend** means 'to grasp, to be or become aware of, to form an idea of', and does not imply full understanding: *I apprehend that what he is trying to do is bankrupt this firm, but I cannot comprehend such stupidity.*

The same distinction applies to **apprehension** and **comprehension**: *The theory of relativity is beyond the comprehension of many people* (i.e. they do not understand what it means) *and beyond the apprehension of animals and insects* (i.e. they are not even aware it exists).

comprise, compose, include

Being similar both in form and in meaning, **comprise** and **compose** are sometimes confused and misused. The difference between them is that a whole comprises its parts, the parts compose the whole: *Great Britain comprises Scotland, England and Wales*; *The three countries which compose Great Britain are Scotland, England and Wales*. **Compose** is often used in the passive: *Water is composed of hydrogen and oxygen*.

Comprise is often used in the passive (e.g. * *Great Britain is comprised of Scotland, England and Wales*) but this is not correct.

Comprise and **include** are sometimes confused, the one being used where the other would be correct. The difference can be seen clearly by considering the following examples: *The book includes chapters on Shakespeare and Milton* (i.e. there are chapters on other people or topics as well); *The book comprises four chapters on Shakespeare and three on Milton* (i.e. these seven chapters constitute the whole book).

concern, concerned

When **concern** and **concerned** convey the notion of anxiety or worry, they may be followed by the prepositions **about** or **over**: *There's no need to concern yourself over what might happen*; *I'm concerned about her lack of progress*. Sometimes **concern(ed)** is followed by **for**, especially when what follows the preposition is something one fears will not happen although one wants it to: *I'm only concerned for her happiness*.

Followed by the prepositions **in** or **with**, **concern(ed)** conveys the idea of involvement or interest rather than anxiety: *Don't concern yourself with unimportant details*; *He shouldn't concern himself in other people's business*.

confident, confidant

The confusion that exists between these two words is more a matter of spelling than of meaning, since the first word is an adjective, the second a noun. **Confident** means 'having a great deal of trust or assurance, having a strong belief', as in *He is confident of winning*; *I'm confident that he will win*. **Confidant** and the feminine form **confidante** mean 'someone in whom you confide, to whom you confide your secrets'.

connection, connexion

Both spellings are acceptable. For further comments, see the article **-ction**, **-xion**.

connoisseur

Note the spelling of this word: two *n*'s, two *s*'s and *oi* between them.

consent see **assent.**

consequent, subsequent, consequential

Consequent usually means 'following as a result', as in *There were rumours of food shortages yesterday and consequent riots in many towns.* **Consequent** may in formal contexts be followed by **on** or **upon**, as in *riots consequent on the rumours of food shortages*, but expressions such as **caused by** or **resulting from** would be more natural in informal contexts.

Consequential is less common than **consequent**. Its most usual meaning is 'important' or, when applied to people, 'self-important' or 'pompous'. In certain formal or technical contexts, it has a meaning similar to that of **consequent**, but whereas **consequent** implies that one thing is a direct result of another, **consequential** implies a less direct link between the two, the one thing logically implying or requiring the other, or in practice giving rise to it, but not actually causing it: *After the riots, there were a number of consequential alterations to the law* (i.e. the riots did not actually cause the changes to the law, but were nonetheless the reason for the changes being made).

Subsequent means 'following, coming after'. It may, but does not always, imply that one thing is a result of another: *his misbehaviour and subsequent dismissal from the firm; At our first meeting, we simply discussed the outlines of the plan; only in subsequent meetings did we look at the details of the project.*

consist

To **consist of** means 'to be composed or made up of', as in *His book consists of nothing more than bits and pieces taken from other people's work.*

To **consist in** is a rather formal expression which means 'to lie in, be contained in, be based on', as in *The beauty of her poetry consists in its very simplicity.*

consistence, consistency see **-ce, -cy nouns.**

constrain, restrain

The verb **constrain** means 'to force, compel'. It is usually used in the passive, as in *You must not feel constrained to go.* **Restrain** means 'to prevent, control, hold back', as in *He had to be restrained from hitting the man; He was so angry, he could hardly restrain himself.*

consult

The verb **consult** means 'to ask for advice or seek information from', as in *You should consult your lawyer*; *He consulted his watch*. To **consult with** means 'to discuss with', as in *He consulted with me about what we should do next*. The use of **consult with** (a person) in the sense given above for the verb **consult** alone is correct in American English but not in British English.

contagious see **infectious**.

contemptible, contemptuous

Contemptible means 'worthy of or deserving contempt'; **contemptuous** means 'showing contempt'.

contiguous see **adjacent**.

continual, continuous

These two adjectives are frequently confused. **Continual** means 'very frequent, happening again and again', as in *I've had continual interruptions all morning*. **Continuous** means 'without a pause or break', as in *continuous rain*. *Continuous noise* is noise that never stops; *continual noise* comes in repeated bursts.

continue

It is wrong to say ***continue on**. Since **continue** on its own means 'to go on, keep on (doing something)', the **on** is redundant.

The verb **continue** may be followed by a verb in **-ing**, by **to** followed by an infinitive, or by **by** plus a verb ending in **-ing**. *She continued to sing 'Waltzing Matilda'* and *She continued singing 'Waltzing Matilda'* means that she already had been singing that song and that she carried on doing so; *She continued by singing 'Waltzing Matilda'* means that she had done something else and then followed that by singing this song.

continuous see **continual**.

controversy

Both *con'troversy* and *controv'ersy* are acceptable pronunciations.

cord, chord

Cord is the only correct spelling for the word which means 'string or cable' or 'a ribbed fabric', as in *They tied his hands with a piece of cord* and *a dress of brown cord*. Both **cord** and **chord** may be used for the parts of the body known as the *vocal cords* and the *spinal cord*, but **cord** is nowadays the preferred form. In the musical and geometrical senses, **chord** alone is correct: *A chord is a number of notes played together; the chord of a circle.*

co-respondent see **correspond.**

corps, corpse

These two words are unlikely to be confused in speech, but may be misspelt when written.

Corps (pronounced [*kōr*]) is 'a number of people working together or carrying out the same duties', as *the diplomatic corps; the medical corps; an army cadet corps.* The plural of **corps** is **corps** (pronounced [*kōrz*]).

A **corpse** (pronounced [*korps*]) is 'a dead body'.

correspond, correspondent

The verb **correspond** may be followed by **to** or **with**. To **correspond to** means 'to be similar or equivalent to', as in *A professor in America corresponds to a university lecturer in Britain.* To **correspond with** means 'to match, be consistent with', as in *His treatment of his staff hardly corresponds with his political ideas.* **Correspond with** is also a formal way of saying 'to write letters to'.

As a point of spelling, note that **correspond** and the related noun **correspondent** have a double *r* between the *o* and the *e*. Do not confuse **correspondent** with **co-respondent**, which is a legal term meaning 'the person who is accused of committing adultery with the husband or wife of a person who is seeking a divorce'.

counsel, council

Counsel is a rather formal word for 'advice'. It is also the legal term for the lawyer or lawyers acting for a person in a law-court: *counsel for the defence.* A **council** is 'a body of people who organize, control, advise, or take decisions': *a county council; The king set up a council of wise men to advise him; a member of the Central Council for Physical Recreation; the Marriage Guidance Council; the Privy Council.*

A **counsellor** is a person who gives advice. A member of a **council** may often be correctly referred to as a **councillor,** especially if the **council** is one of the various bodies of people elected to control the workings of local government in counties, regions, etc.: *a local councillor.* However, if the function of a **council** is to give advice, its members will more correctly be referred to as **counsellors**: *the king's wise counsellors; marriage guidance counsellors; Privy Counsellors (Privy Councillors* is also correct). Often when a **council** is simply an executive or organizing committee, its members are referred to simply as 'members of the council'.

course see **coarse.**

credible, credulous, creditable
Credible means 'believable': *a scarcely credible story.* **Credulous** means 'too easily convinced, too ready to believe, easily fooled', as in *Only someone as credulous as Peter could believe a story like that.* **Creditable** means 'worthy of praise or respect', as in *Although he didn't win, he gave a creditable performance in the competition.*

-ction, -xion
Most words ending in [-*ak′shən*], [-*ek′shən*], [-*ik′shən*], etc. are spelt **-ction**:

action	*deflection*	*fraction*	*protection*
conduction	*dejection*	*friction*	*putrefaction*
confection	*distraction*	*infection*	*reflection*
connection	*election*	*inflection*	*section*
contraction	*erection*	*inspection*	
conviction	*fiction*	*introduction*	

Similarly, with an *n* before the *c*:

conjunction	*disjunction*	*distinction*	*extinction*

In British English, but not American English, four of the words in the above list may be written **-xion**:

connexion	*deflexion*	*inflexion*	*reflexion*

The **-ction** forms are now commoner than the **-xion** forms, but some people still prefer the forms *connexion* and *inflexion*.
A few words must be written **-xion.** Among these are *complexion* and *crucifixion*.

curb see **kerb.**

currant, current
Care must be taken with the spelling of these words. A **currant** is a fruit. A **current** is a flow of air, water, or electricity. **Current** is also the spelling of the adjective, as in *current affairs*.

customer, client, clientele
The essential difference between a **customer** and a **client** is that a **customer** buys something (e.g. in a shop) whereas a **client** receives a service (e.g. professional advice) from someone (such as a lawyer). The distinction is not, however, absolute: a hair-dresser, for example, may have **customers** or **clients**, and **client** is sometimes used as a supposedly more polite or more formal synonym of **customer**, which it isn't.
Clientele is a collective noun for **clients** or **customers** (see **collective noun**).

-cy nouns see **-ce.**

cynic(al), sceptic(al)

A **cynic** is a person who has a low opinion of human nature, who thinks the worst about everyone and everything, and who believes that behind something apparently good there must be lurking something unpleasant or undesirable: *He's such a cynic, he thinks that people who work for a charity must be stealing half the money they collect.* **Cynical** means 'of, like, or showing that one is, a cynic': *a cynical attitude to politics and politicians.*

A **sceptic** is a person who believes that nothing can be known with absolute certainty, or, more loosely, a person who is unwilling to believe some particular statement, theory, etc.: *Most people now accept this hypothesis, but there are still a few sceptics.* **Sceptical** means 'of, like, or showing that one is, a sceptic': *They do say that apples help to clean your teeth, but I'm a bit sceptical about that.*

dare

When the verb **dare** means 'to challenge (someone to do something)', it is followed by **to** and an infinitive: *I dare you to say that to her; Even if he dares you to do it, don't do it.*

When **dare** means 'to be brave enough to', it may be used with any of three constructions:

1. It may be followed by **to** and an infinitive, just as it is in the sense of 'to challenge' above: *I do not dare to criticize him; Will he dare to come?; If he dares to do that, I'll smack him.*

2. It may be followed by an infinitive without **to**: *I do not dare criticize him; Will he dare come?; If he dares do that, I'll smack him.*

3. **Dare** may behave as an auxiliary verb (like **can**, **will**, **must**), in which case it is again followed by an infinitive without **to**: *I dare not criticize him; Daren't he come?; If he dare do that, I'll smack him.* (Note that in this third type of construction, with **dare** as an auxiliary verb, the third person singular is **dare**, not **dares**.)

The phrase **dare say** (= to expect, suppose, agree) is now normally written as two words, but it may also be written as a single word. It is only used with the pronoun **I** and in the present tense: *I dare say/daresay you're right.*

dash

A dash is sometimes used along with a colon to introduce a list, especially if the list begins on a new line, but this is deprecated by many people and a colon alone is usually quite sufficient. A dash should certainly not be used when the list immediately follows

49

the colon on the same line, as in *We need to buy various things: potatoes, cheese, eggs, butter, and flour* (not * ... *things:— potatoes,* ...).

Like a colon, a dash may be used to introduce an explanation or expansion of something preceding it, as in *These are the characteristics of a good play — the characters should be believable, the action gripping, and the ending unexpected.* Two dashes may be used to mark a parenthesis or an aside, as in *His new car — a Rover, I believe — cost over £7000.* In general, the use of dashes rather than colons or brackets in such cases gives a more informal tone to what is written.

A dash is used to introduce a summing-up of what has preceded, as in *Believable characters, gripping action, and an unexpected ending — these are the main characteristics of a good play.* And if a sentence is broken off in the middle, a dash marks the break, as in *What really annoys me is that she — but then, what's the use of talking about it?*

data

Strictly speaking, **data** is a plural noun (the singular form **datum** is only rarely used), but in modern English, there is an increasing tendency to regard **data** as a collective noun (see **collective noun**) and to follow it with a singular verb: *The data has been gathered from many sources.* Although some purists still abhor this use, it is acceptable to most people nowadays, and must now therefore be considered correct usage.

dates

The two most frequently used styles for writing dates are *6 November 1984* and *November 6th 1984*. Both styles are correct, but the former is much the commoner nowadays, especially on formal and business letters. Note that in the first style, the date-number need not be followed by *st, nd, rd* or *th*, i.e. *6 November*, but *6th November* is not wrong; *st*, etc. are, however, required if the day is not followed by the month: *I saw him on the 6th.* Note also that no commas are required in dates; some people do prefer to insert one after the day in the second style above – thus *November 6th, 1984* – but while not wrong, this is quite unnecessary. If, however, the day of the week precedes a date, it <u>should</u> be followed by a comma: *Tuesday, 6 November 1984.*

The whole date may be written in numbers (e.g. *6/11/84* or *6.11.84*) but this is best avoided in formal or business contexts as it can lead to confusion: in British English *6.11.84* means *6 November 1984*, but in American English it would be understood as *11 June 1984*.

When pairs of years are linked by a dash, it is normal only to give as much of the second year as is required for clarity:

1975 to 1983 can be written *1975-83*

1982 to 1984 can be written *1982-4*

Exceptions to this rule are the numbers from 10 to 19, which are written out in full whether clarity requires it or not:

1914 to 1918 is written *1914-18*, not **1914-8*.

If the linked dates are in different centuries, write out the second date in full:

1892 to 1905 is written *1892-1905*, not **1892-905*.

Note that if you are using *A.D.* and *B.C.*, *B.C.* follows the year, but *A.D.* precedes it: *44B.C.*; *A.D. 44*.

Since the first century A.D. began with the year 1 and ended with the year 100, the nineteenth century began in 1801 and ended in 1900, and the twentieth century began in the year 1901. A common mistake is to think of a century beginning, rather than ending, in a -00 year.

decimate

Decimate originally meant 'to kill one in ten of'. Its meaning has now widened to 'to kill a large number of or destroy a large part of', as in *The population was decimated by the plague*. It should not, however, be used when complete destruction or annihilation is meant: when something is decimated, a part of it – be it a large or a small part – remains unharmed.

defective, deficient

The adjective **defective** means 'having a fault or flaw': *a defective machine*. **Deficient** means 'inadequate, lacking in what is needed': *Their food is deficient in vitamins*.

defence, defense see -ce, -se.

deficient see defective.

definite, definitive

These words are not synonymous. **Definite** means 'clear' or 'certain': *I'll give you a definite answer later*. **Definitive** means 'final, settling things once and for all': *He has written the definitive study of Ben Jonson*.

delusion, illusion, allusion

Delusion and **illusion** are often confused because of their similarity in meaning, **illusion** and **allusion** because of their similarity in sound and spelling.

A **delusion** is a false belief which is completely accepted as being the truth: *He is suffering from the delusion that he is Jesus Christ.* An **illusion** is a false impression, or something which causes a false impression, which is accepted only provisionally or temporarily (until further experience provides counter-evidence), or perhaps not accepted or believed at all: *She used to believe that all politicians were honest, but a series of scandals shattered her illusions; The lines he had drawn did not look parallel, but he knew that was only an optical illusion.* That a magician appears to saw a person in half is an **illusion**; to believe that he actually does do so would be to suffer from a **delusion**.

An **allusion** is a passing hint at or indirect reference to (something): *Classical Chinese poetry is often difficult to understand because of the many allusions to people and things modern readers know nothing about.*

demand

The verb **demand** in the sense of 'to order' may be followed by **that**: *I demand that you do it at once.* In the sense of 'to ask for', it is followed by **to** plus a verb or **from** plus a noun or pronoun: *I demand to know what is going on; I demand an explanation from you.* In the sense of 'to require, need', it is followed by **of**: *This job demands a lot of you.*

The noun **demand** may be followed by **for** or **on**. In the sense of 'request, desire', it is followed by **for**: *There is no demand for a product like that.* In the sense of 'requirement of effort, etc.', **demand** is followed by **on**: *This job makes a lot of demands on my time.*

deny see **refute**.

depend

Depend is normally followed by **on** or **upon**: *It all depends on what you mean by correct English.* In informal speech, it may correctly be used without the preposition, as in *It depends what you mean*, but this non-prepositional construction should not be used in formal speech and writing.

dependant, dependent

In British English, **dependant** is a noun meaning 'a person who is supported by another' and **dependent** is an adjective meaning 'depending (on)'. In American English, both the noun and the adjective are generally spelt **dependent**.

dependence, dependency see **-ce, -cy nouns**.

deprecate, depreciate

Deprecate is a formal word meaning 'to disapprove of, express disapproval of', as in *The government issued a statement deprecating the soldiers' actions*. To **depreciate**, which is often confused with **deprecate**, means 'to fall in value', 'to reduce the value of', 'to speak of as having little value or importance', as in *Shares have depreciated recently*; *Modesty is one thing, but you should not depreciate your abilities the way you do*.

derisive, derisory

Formerly these words were synonymous, but they are no longer so: **derisive** means 'mocking, showing derision', as in *derisive laughter*; **derisory** means 'ridiculous, deserving derision or mockery', as in *a derisory offer/amount*.

desert, dessert

Deserts (pronounced [*dez'ərts*]) are areas of hot, dry, barren country. Pronounced [*di-zûrts'*], **deserts** are what someone deserves; this word almost always occurs nowadays in the phrase *to get one's (just) deserts* 'to suffer the (usually bad) fate one deserves'. **Dessert** (pronounced [*di-zûrt'*]) is the sweet course of a meal: *We had strawberries and cream for dessert*.

diaphragm

Note the spelling of this word, especially the *ph* and the *g*. Note also that the *g* is not pronounced: the word is [*dī'ə-fram*].

diarrhoea

A word often misspelt. Note the double *r*, the *h*, and the *oe*.

differ

To **differ from** is 'to be different from', as in *Her house differs from mine in that it has the staircase at the front*. To **differ with** is a rather formal way of saying 'to disagree with', as in *He differs with me over the value of nuclear weapons*.

different

Contrary to what many people believe, both **different from** and **different to** are correct English. **Different than** is less acceptable than **different from/to**, permissible in informal speech but best avoided in formal speech and writing.

dilemma

Strictly speaking, a **dilemma** is not just any problem or difficulty, but a situation in which one is faced with having to choose between two possible courses of action, both unpleasant, undesirable or unsatisfactory. The word may be applied to situations in which there are more than two possible courses of action but should not be used when there is only one, and the possibilities should always be things one would wish to avoid.

dinner see **lunch**.

diphtheria, diphthong

Note the *phth* in the spelling of these words. Note also that the correct pronunciation is [*dif-*], not [*dip-*].

disc, disk

Disc is now the preferred spelling in British English, but **disk** is still found, especially in works relating to computers and computer science: this may be due to the influence of American English, which prefers the form **disk**.

discrete, discreet

Discrete and **discreet** derive from the same Latin word, but in English they are different words with separate meanings: **discreet** means 'prudent, cautious, not saying or doing anything that might cause trouble', as in *My secretary won't ask awkward questions, she is very discreet*, whereas **discrete** means 'separate, not attached to others', as in *a suspension of discrete particles in a liquid*. Note that **discretion** means 'discreetness', not 'discreteness'.

diseases

Diseases such as *measles*, *mumps* and *shingles*, although plural in form, are treated as singular nouns in English: *Measles is a disease that people usually get in childhood*.

disinterested, uninterested

The adjective **disinterested** is often used where **uninterested** would be correct. **Uninterested** means 'not interested, not showing any interest'. **Disinterested** means 'not biased, not influenced by private feelings or selfish motives', as in *I think we need the opinions of a few disinterested observers*.

disk see **disc**.

distinct, distinctive

These adjectives are sometimes confused. **Distinct** means 'clearly or easily seen, heard, smelt, etc': *a distinct smell of alcohol*; *There is a distinct Scottishness in her pronunciation*. **Distinctive** means 'characteristic, distinguishing one person or thing from others', as in *She has a very distinctive walk*; *the distinctive call of a barn owl*.

distrust, mistrust

Distrust and **mistrust** are virtually synonymous, but **distrust**

usually suggests a greater doubt, suspicion or lack of trust than
mistrust.

disturb see **perturb.**

do

Do is often used in English to avoid the repetition of a verb or
verb-phrase, as in *He enjoys that as much as I do* (= as much as I
enjoy it). There are, however, certain constructions in which the
use of **do** is not correct, and care must be taken to avoid these:

1.   **Do** should not be used as a substitute for a verb which has
not actually been used already but has only been implied. In
**No reply was forthcoming although they had promised they would do*,
do replaces an implied verb *reply* which does not appear any-
where in the sentence (*reply* in the example is a noun); it would
be better to say . . .*promised to reply* or . . .*promised they would
reply.*

2.   Particular care must be taken to ensure that **do** and the
previous occurrence of the verb it replaces agree with regard to
active or passive voice. A sentence such as **John was laughed at
by the girls this morning just as we did last night* is not correct
because *was laughed at* is a passive verb and *did* is in an active
verb. The sentence must be recast to make both verbs active
or both passive, e.g. *The girls laughed at John* . . .or . . .*just as he
was by us last night.*

3.   **Do** should not be used as a substitute for the verb **be**: **He
told me to be careful but I didn't* is not correct; say . . .*but I wasn't.*

4.   In informal English, **do** may be used as a substitute for
the verb **have** or for a verb in a tense formed with **have**, as in *I
have more difficulty with English grammar than you do* and *I have read
more books than he has done.* Such constructions are not approved
of by some people and are best avoided in formal speech and
writing, where . . .*than you have* and . . .*than he has* would be
better in the above sentences.

doctor, physician, surgeon

The general word for a person who has been trained to diagnose
and treat people's illnesses is **doctor**. A **physician** is a rather
formal or technical word for a doctor who specializes in the use
of medicines rather than surgery in the treatment of patients,
especially at a hospital. A **surgeon** is a doctor specializing in the
use of surgical operations to treat patients.

Note that a person who uses the title **Doctor** may either be a
medical doctor or have received the degree of Doctor of Philoso-

phy, Doctor of Literature, Doctor of Theology, etc. from a university.

double negatives

Constructions with two negative words which are equivalent in meaning to a single negative are not correct in standard English (although quite permissible in some non-standard forms of English). A sentence like *I never did nothing* is ungrammatical if what is meant is 'I never did anything'. A similar double-negative construction is sometimes heard in statements of surprise or wonder, as for example *I shouldn't be surprised if it didn't rain this afternoon*, but although such expressions may be heard even in the speech of educated people who would deny that they ever used double negatives, they are no more logical or grammatical than *I never did nothing* and should therefore be avoided: say, rather, *I shouldn't be surprised if it rained*.

Of course, if *I never did nothing* means 'There was never a time when I did nothing', the use of the two negatives is quite correct, as here both words carry their full negative meaning. Similarly, two negative words may be used together in a sentence as a stylistic device, e.g. to make a less forceful statement than the corresponding positive word would: *I was not disinclined to go* means 'I was quite inclined to go'.

Care must be taken not to use so many negative words in a sentence that the meaning of the sentence becomes obscure or distorted. Particular attention must be paid to words such as **hardly**, **scarcely**, **without**, etc. which are negative in force but not in form: they also may appear in double-negative constructions which are often less easy to spot than the 'I never did nothing' type of construction, as for example *He hadn't scarcely a penny in the bank* and *I don't believe hardly anything he tells me*, which correctly should be *He had scarcely a penny in the bank* and *I believe hardly anything he tells me*.

doubt, doubtful

When **doubt** and **doubtful** are part of a positive statement they may be followed by **whether**, **if** or **that**. **Whether** is more often used than **if** in formal speech and writing, and **that** is best restricted to informal contexts. In a negative statement or a question, **doubt** and **doubtful** should be followed by **that**. The following examples show the correct usage: *I doubt whether/if he is coming*; (informal) *I doubt that he is coming*; *I am doubtful whether he is coming*; *I do not doubt that he is coming*; *There is no doubt that he is coming*; *Do you doubt that he is coming?*

downward, downwards

Both **downward** and **downwards** may be used as adverbs, the form with *s* being the commoner in British English, the form without *s* normal in American English.

Only **downward** is correct as an adjective: *a downward curve/tendency.*

draft, draught

In British English, a **draft** is 'a rough sketch or outline' (*a rough draft of my speech*) or 'an order to a bank for the payment of money' (*a bank draft for £40*). A **draught** is 'a current of air', 'a quantity of liquid drunk at one time' (*He took a long draught of beer*), 'the amount of water a boat requires to float' (*This boat has a shallow draught*), 'beer taken from a barrel' (*draught beer*), and 'one of the pieces used in the game of *draughts*'.

In American English, **draft** is the normal spelling for all the above meanings.

drunk, drunken

Drunk means 'suffering from the effects of having drunk too much alcohol', as in *That man is drunk; a drunk man.* It may also be used as a noun: *There are too many drunks around these days.* When used before a noun, **drunken** may mean the same as **drunk**, as in *a drunken man* (though this is now less common than *a drunk man*) or it may mean 'caused by a person's having drunk too much alcohol', as in *a drunken brawl/stupor.* **Drunken** may also be used to mean 'in the habit of becoming drunk', as in *her drunken husband*, and in this sense it need not be followed by a noun: *Her husband is drunken and dissolute.*

due to see because of.

dying, dyeing

Dying is the present participle of the verb **to die**, as in *He is dying of cancer*; **dyeing** is the present participle of the verb **to dye**, as in *They are dyeing their shirts and socks red.*

each

When **each** precedes the word to which it refers, it should be followed by a singular verb: *Each child has six pencils; Each of the children has six pencils.* When **each** follows the word it refers to, it should be followed by a plural verb: *The children each have six pencils.*

Each refers to members of a group. When the emphasis is on the group as a whole, **each** precedes the main describing word (verb or adjective) of the sentence and pronouns, etc. occurring later in the sentence refer to the whole group, as in *We are each responsible for our own children* in which **each** precedes the adjective *responsible* and the possessive *our* refers to the whole group described by the pronoun *we*. On the other hand, when the emphasis is on each member of the group as an individual, **each** follows the main descriptive word, and subsequent pronouns, etc. refer back to each member of the group individually, as in *We are responsible each for his own children*.

each other, one another

Some people prefer to use **each other** when referring to two people or things, and **one another** when more than two are involved, as in *The two children helped each other* and *The four children helped one another*. Although some authorities insist on this rule, this supposed difference between **each other** and **one another** is not, and never has been, a rule of English grammar, and there is no reason to abide by it.

economic, economical

Economic means 'pertaining to economics' or 'pertaining to the economy of a country, etc.', as in *economic history*; *the country's economic future*. It also means 'giving an adequate profit or fair return', as in *We must charge an economic rent/price*. **Economical** means 'thrifty', 'not wasteful, expensive, or extravagant', as in *This car is very economical on petrol*; *economical use of supplies*.

-ed in adjectives and adverbs

When the suffix **-ed** is added to a verb to form a past participle it is pronounced [*-id*] when it follows the sounds [*t*] and [*d*], [*t*] after [*p, t, k, f, th, sh, ch*], and [*d*] after all other consonants and all vowels: consider, for example, the pronunciation of *added*, *talked*, *watched*, *used*, *applied*, etc. Adjectives of a similar form do not obey this rule: consider the pronunciation of *naked*, *rugged*, *wicked*, *wretched*, etc. Generally, when past participles are used as adjectives, their pronunciation does not alter: *added attractions*; *a used car*; *applied science*. However, there are a number of adjectives corresponding to, or at least identical in form to, past participles, whose final syllable is pronounced [*id*] contrary to what one might expect. Among the commonest of these are *aged* (as in *an aged man*), *beloved*, *blessed*, *crooked*, *dogged*, *jagged*, *learned* (as in *a learned professor*) and *ragged*.

A change in pronunciation similar to the one described above is seen in certain adverbs. Although the adjectives *advised*, *alleged*, *avowed, deserved, fixed* are pronounced with [*d*] and *marked* with [*t*], the corresponding adverbs are pronounced with [*id*], as *advisedly* (pronounced [*əd-vīz'id-li*]), *markedly* (pronounced [*märk'id-li*]), etc. This change in pronunciation occurs in adverbs formed from adjectives in which the syllable before the **-ed** suffix is stressed.

-ed, -t in verbs see **-t.**

effect see **affect.**

effective, effectual, efficacious, efficient

These four words all have meanings relating to 'the producing of desired results', but they are not synonyms.

Effective and **effectual** are almost synonymous, but **effectual** puts more emphasis on the actual achievement of the result than does **effective**, which may mean 'producing results' or 'able or likely to produce results': if the police take *effective* measures to combat the rising crime rate, these measures either are having the desired effect, or are expected to, whereas if they take *effectual* measures, there is no doubt that these measures are succeeding in reducing the crime rate.

Efficacious is nowadays applied only to medicines and medical treatment. It means 'producing the intended result (i.e. cure)'.

Efficient applies more to the way in which a result is achieved rather than to the result itself. It means 'producing results competently, without wasting time, effort, etc.', as in *efficient methods*; *an efficient secretary*.

egoist, egotist

These words are the cause of much confusion and uncertainty. Strictly speaking, an **egotist** is a person who is too preoccupied with himself, who is self-important and vain, and who uses 'I' and 'me' too much in speaking, whereas **egoist** is a technical philosophical term for a person who believes that the only thing one can be certain of is one's own existence, or that self-interest is the correct basis of morality. If a person is simply selfish, he is an **egotist**; if his selfishness is based on the philosophical principle of self-interest, he is an **egoist**.

Egoist is often used where **egotist** would correctly convey the intended meaning, but the distinction between these words is useful and worth maintaining.

either

Either is followed by a singular verb: *I don't think that either of them* *is capable of doing it*; *Either one suits me*. **Either** can only be used when referring to one or other of <u>two</u> people, things, etc.; if the reference is to more than two, **any** must be used.

There are two points to be noted in particular with regard to words or phrases linked by **either . . . or**:

1. If **either . . . or** links two singular words that are the subjects of a verb, the verb is singular, but if one of the words is plural, so also is the verb: *Either John or Mary is wrong*; *Either John or his friends are wrong*.

2. Care must be taken to ensure that the words or phrases which follow **either** and **or** match in construction. In **You may either send John or his brother*, **either** is followed by a verb plus its object, **or** by an object alone; the correct construction would be *You may send either John or his brother*, with both **either** and **or** followed by an object of the verb.

elder, older

The normal comparative and superlative forms of the adjective **old** are **older** and **oldest**. **Elder** and **eldest** are now used only to describe relative seniority within a family, as in *He is my elder brother*; *Her eldest son is at university*. **Older**, rather than **elder**, must be used even for family relationships in comparative constructions with **than**, as *My brother is older than me*, not ** . . . elder than me*. **Elder** also occurs in a few idioms, such as *elder statesman*.

electric, electrical, electronic

The adjective **electric** should be used when one is referring to something which is powered by, which is caused by, or which produces, electricity: *an electric shock*; *an electric light*; *an electric eel*. **Electrical** means 'pertaining generally to electricity or things connected with electricity', as in *electrical engineering*; *the electrical department of a shop*. **Electrical**, rather than **electric**, is used when referring to general classes of things powered by electricity rather than to specific types of thing: <u>*Electric*</u> *kettles and* <u>*electric*</u> *irons are examples of* <u>*electrical*</u> *goods*.

Electronic is used of sophisticated electrical apparatus, such as television sets or computers, in which the electric current is controlled by valves, transistors or the like. It is also applied to the use or production of such equipment: *electronic engineering*.

embarrass

Note the double *r* and the double *s*.

emend see amend.

eminent, imminent

Eminent means 'outstanding, distinguished, famous', as in *an eminent lawyer*. **Imminent** means 'likely to happen very soon', and is very often used of unpleasant or undesirable things, as in *imminent danger*; *A storm is imminent*.

-ence see -ance, -ant.

encyclopaedia, encyclopedia

Both forms of this word are correct, but the former is still the commoner one in British English.

end

To **end in** means 'to have (something) as its end or at its end', as in *The word 'president' ends in -ent*; *The path ended in a farmyard*; *The branch ends in a number of feathery leaves*. **End** followed by **in** also means 'to have as a result', as in *The disagreement at the factory ended in a strike*. **End by** or **end with** means 'to do (something) at the end', as in *He ended by singing a song* or *He ended his act with a song*.

English

The adjective **English** is often incorrectly used to mean 'belonging to, being a citizen of, Great Britain or the United Kingdom'. The Scots, the Welsh and the people of Northern Ireland are not English. **English** correctly means only 'belonging to, being a citizen of, England'.

enormity, enormousness

Of these two nouns, only **enormousness** should be used when referring to size. **Enormity** means 'great wickedness, serious crime', as in *the enormity of his assault on the little girl*. **Enormity** is sometimes used as a synonym of **enormousness**, but this is best avoided as it is not generally considered correct.

enquire, inquire

To most people **enquire** and **inquire**, and **enquiry** and **inquiry**, are simply alternative spellings. There are some who maintain that **enquire** and **enquiry** are to be preferred when all that is meant is a simple asking and **inquire/inquiry** when a more detailed investigation is meant, but this distinction is not recognized by many authorities on English and is not adhered to by many speakers of English, although in phrases such as *court of inquiry*, which imply a detailed investigation, **inquiry** is the form normally used, not **enquiry**.

ensure see insure.

-ent see **-ance, -ant.**

equable, equitable

The adjective **equable** means 'not extreme and without great variation', as in *Britain has an equable climate*. It also means 'even-tempered', as in *That child would infuriate the most equable person*. **Equitable** is a rather formal word which means 'fair, just', as in *Distribute the money in an equitable way*.

equally as

Equally should not be used with **as**, as in *This one is equally as good. Use either **equally** or **as** alone, or **just as**: *This one is equally good*; *This one is just as good*.

-er, -or, -ar

The suffix **-er** can be added to verbs in English to form words meaning 'someone who —s': *singer, builder, worker, talker*, etc. If the verb ends in *e*, the *e* is dropped before **-er** is added: *smoker, writer, baker*. If the final consonant of the verb doubles in forming the present participle, it does so also before the **-er** suffix: *swim, swimming, swimmer; run, running, runner*.

A number of 'doer' words end in **-or**: among the commonest of these are *actor, censor, conqueror, counsellor, duplicator, incubator, inspector, prospector, sailor, supervisor, survivor*, and also (not related directly to verbs) *author, chancellor, councillor, doctor*.

With some verb roots, both **-er** and **-or** forms are possible, forming words with different meanings: compare *resister* 'one who resists' and *resistor* 'a piece of electrical apparatus'.

Note that two common words are spelt with **-ar**: *liar* and *beggar*.

especially, specially

These two words are often treated as synonyms, but their meanings are not the same. **Especially** means 'particularly', as in *These insects are quite common, especially in hot countries; I was especially pleased to meet him*. **Specially** means 'for a special purpose', as in *I made this cake specially for your birthday*. **Specially** is sometimes used in the sense of **especially**, but it is best to keep the meanings separate as outlined above.

-ess

Many of the feminine words ending in **-ess** are now rare or obsolete, but others are still generally used. The following is a list of the commonest **-ess** words still in current use: *abbess, actress, countess, deaconess, duchess, hostess, lioness, manageress* (of a shop), *mayoress* (the wife of a mayor or a lady mayor), *princess, stewardess, tigress,* *waitress*. Among those now rarely if ever used are *authoress, editress, Jewess, Negress, poetess, sculptress, shepherdess*.

Notice that when **-ess** is added to certain words, the vowel of the preceding syllable is dropped: *actor, actress; tiger, tigress; waiter, waitress*.

even

Careful attention must be paid to the placing of the adverb **even** in a sentence, as its position affects the meaning of the whole sentence. **Even** should, at least in written English, stand immediately before the word or words in a sentence which it is meant to emphasize, as in the following sentences:

Even John helped me (= of all people, I did not expect John to help me, but he did).

John even helped me (= he didn't just watch or offer advice).

John helped even me (= he didn't just help other people, but me as well).

In spoken English, stress and intonation patterns help to convey the meaning intended, and **even** is frequently placed before the verb even when it is modifying some other word or phrase in the sentence. In *John even helped me* (with stress on *me*), it is clear that **even** is modifying *me* even though it is standing before *helped*. Similarly in *John even helped me* (with stress on *John*) it is clear that **even** is modifying *John*.

ever, -ever

When **ever** is used to emphasize words like *why, how, where*, etc., it is written as a separate word: *What ever shall I do?*; *How ever did you manage that?* When **ever** means 'any — at all', it is joined to the word it modifies as a suffix: *You may do whatever you please*; *Go wherever he tells you to go*. Notice that **where ever**, **why ever**, etc. are questions, **wherever**, **whatever**, etc. parts of statements or commands.

In British English, **for ever** is more often written as two words than one, but **forever** is also correct. Some people make a distinction between **forever** meaning 'continually' and **for ever** meaning 'for all time' but, while such a distinction has much to recommend it, it is not recognized by most dictionaries or speakers of English. In American English, **forever** is the standard form.

every

Every is followed by a singular verb: *Every room is painted white*; *Not every family has a car*.

every one, everyone

Every one means 'each individual one', and can apply to people or things: *I examined all the cups, and found that every one had a flaw in it*. **Everyone** means 'every person, all people (thought of as a group rather than as individuals)': *Everyone thinks I'm crazy*; *Everyone in this street owns a car*.

exaggerate

This is a word that is often misspelt. Note the *gg*.

exclamation mark

An exclamation mark is used in place of a full stop to indicate an exclamation or sentence expressing strong emotion. It should not normally be used after a command unless it is needed for particular emphasis.

An exclamation mark in parentheses is sometimes used to draw attention to something one finds surprising in a statement. It should be placed immediately after the word or words one wants to draw attention to, as in *Although he said he enjoyed(!) being ill, he was clearly depressed that morning*.

faeces

Note the *ae* in the spelling of this word.

farther see **further.**

fascinated, fascination

Fascinated may be followed by **by** or **with**: *He's fascinated by/with motorbikes*. **Fascination** in the sense of 'being fascinated' may be followed by **for** or **with**, as in *his fascination with/for motorbikes*, and by **for** alone in the sense 'causing fascination', as in *Motorbikes have a great fascination for him*.

fatal, fateful

The adjective **fateful** is sometimes used when **fatal** is what is meant. **Fatal** means 'causing death or disaster', as in *a fatal accident*; *She made the fatal mistake of telling him what she thought*. **Fateful** means 'of great importance, involving important decisions, having important results, etc.', as in *At last the fateful day arrived, the day she was to be married*.

February

The name of this month is often misspelt. Note the *r* and the *u*.

feel

To **feel for** is 'to be sympathetic towards, understand the feelings of', as in *She felt for him in his sorrow.* It also means 'to try to find by feeling', as in *She felt for the light-switch.* To **feel like** is 'to want, feel that one would like to have, do, etc. (something)', as in *I feel like a drink*; *Do you feel like going to the cinema?*, or 'to feel as if one was (something)', as in *I feel like a princess.*

female, feminine

The adjective **female** means 'of the sex that gives birth to children, produces eggs or seeds, etc.' and may be applied to people, animals, plants, or anything that has sexual differences between members of the species: *A female pig is called a sow.* **Feminine** can only be applied to people (men or women), and means 'characteristic of a woman, having the qualities or characteristics one would expect or wish for in a woman': *He has a rather feminine voice.*

few, a few

Few and **a few** both mean 'not many', but they are not synonymous: **few** emphasizes the negative side of the situation, the smallness of the number, **a few** the positive side, the fact that there are indeed some: *There are few honest politicians these days but I suppose we must be grateful that there are still a few.*

fewer, less

Fewer and **less** are not interchangeable: **fewer** should be used when reference is being made to numbers of individuals, **less** when an amount or quantity is denoted. **Fewer** is followed by or linked to a plural noun: *I grew fewer leeks this year*; *Fewer boys than girls want to become nurses.* **Less** is normally followed by a singular noun, but may be followed by a plural noun if that noun is thought of as denoting an amount rather than a number of individuals: *There is less water in this bottle than in that one*; *The stew needs less salt and more pepper*; *He earns less than £500 per month* (compare *There were fewer than 500 people at the match*).

fight with

Notice that **fight with** is ambiguous: it can mean both 'fight against' and 'fight on the same side as'. If you use this phrase, make sure your meaning is clear.

flagrant, blatant

Flagrant implies a greater degree of condemnation than **blatant**. **Blatant** means 'glaringly or shamelessly obvious': *a blatant lie*. **Flagrant** means 'scandalous, very obvious and wicked': *flagrant dishonesty.*

flammable, inflammable

Flammable and **inflammable** mean the same thing, 'able or likely to burn' but not a few accidents have been caused by people thinking that **inflammable** meant 'not flammable'. **Inflammable** is the form normally used in everyday situations, **flammable** the form preferred in technical contexts. The opposites of these words are **non-flammable** and **non-inflammable**.

flaunt, flout

These two words are often confused, although their meanings are not at all similar. To **flaunt** something is 'to show (something) off, display (something) ostentatiously', as in *She was flaunting her new fur coat in front of her colleagues*. **Flout** means 'to treat (something) with contempt, to refuse to obey or comply with (something)', as in *He flouts authority/the law/his mother's wishes*.

for-, fore-

The prefix **for-** means 'away', 'not', 'against', 'utterly', but it is not a living prefix and its meaning is not always obvious in words which begin with it, such as *forget* and *forgive*. Other common words beginning with **for-** are *forbear, forbid, forgo, forlorn, forsake*, and *forswear*.

The prefix **fore-** means 'before, in front, beforehand'. It is much commoner than **for-**, and there are a great many words beginning with this prefix, among which are *forearm, foreboding, forecast, forefinger, forehead, forerunner, foresee, foreshadow, forestall, foretell*, and *forewarn*.

A few of the words beginning with **for-** and **fore-** are very similar, and especial attention must be paid to these: to *forbear* is 'not to do (something)', a *forebear* is 'an ancestor' (the spelling *forbear* is also correct); to *forgo* means 'to do without (something)', a *foregone conclusion* is 'an obvious or inevitable conclusion'. Notice also the difference in spelling between the *foreword* of a book and the adverb *forward*.

for ever, forever see **ever**.

former, latter

Former should only be used to refer to the first, and **latter** to the second, of two people or things just mentioned. In referring to items or individuals in larger groups, use **first**, **second**, **last**, etc.

fortunate, fortuitous

Fortunate means 'lucky'; **fortuitous** means 'accidental, occurring by chance'.

forward, forwards

As adverbs, both **forward** and **forwards** are correct, but the two forms of the word are not interchangeable in all contexts. **Forwards** is now only used when actual movement or direction is meant, as in *He walked forwards slowly through the mist.* **Forward** may also be used in this sense, as in *She stepped forward to receive her prize.* In other senses, i.e. when there is no notion of direction involved, only **forward** may be used, never **forwards**: *from this time forward*; *They will consider the suggestion that you put forward*; *They have brought forward the date of their wedding.*

The adjective form, meaning 'at or to the front, advancing', is always **forward**: *a forward movement*; *the forward part of a ship.*

frightened

When **frightened** denotes 'being in a long-lasting or permanent state of fear', it is followed by the preposition **of**, as in *He is frightened of dogs*; *She is frightened of being alone in the house*, or by **to** plus a verb, as in *She is frightened to be alone in the house.*

Frightened of may also denote a state of fear at a particular time, as in *I'm frightened of that big dog over there.* If the emphasis is on the sudden causing of a state of fear, **frightened** is followed by **by**: *While walking in the park, he was frightened by a large dog.*

If **frightened** is used to refer to a state of fear which prevents one doing something, it is followed by **to** plus a verb, as in *He was frightened to say what he was really thinking.*

If **frightened** means 'in a state of anxiety or fear about something one has to or might have to do', it is followed by **at**, generally with nouns such as **thought**, **idea** or **notion**, as in *He was frightened at the thought of having to chair the meeting.*

In colloquial English, **frightened** may also be followed by **about** when it is used of a short-lived state of fear at a particular time in the present or future: *There's nothing to be frightened about — the doctor won't hurt you.*

-ful

The correct plural of words formed with **-ful**, such as *cupful*, *handful*, *spoonful* and so on, is **-fuls**, not **-sful*: *three spoonfuls* is correct, **three spoonsful* is wrong.

fulfil

Note that this word is not spelt **fullfil*. In American English, the correct spelling is **fulfill**.

full stop

A **full stop**, or **period**, is used to mark the end of a sentence. For the use of full stops with abbreviations, see **abbreviations**.

further, farther

Further is now commoner than **farther**. **Farther** may only be used when there is an actual sense of 'distance' involved in the meaning, as in *I cannot walk any farther*. **Further** may also be used in this sense, and must be used when the sense is 'more', 'additional', 'beyond this stage', etc., as in *I would like to make a further point*; *further education*; *closed until further notice*. **Further**, and not **farther**, is also used as a verb meaning 'to help to proceed towards success, completion, etc.', as in *This will further his promotion prospects*.

fused participle

Fused participle is the name given to a construction consisting of a noun or pronoun plus a present participle (the '-ing' form of a verb) together acting as the subject of a verb or the object of a verb or preposition, as in *I insisted on <u>them removing</u> the picture*; *<u>You laughing</u> like that worries me*. Some purists condemn this construction, preferring instead the use of a possessive (*I insisted on <u>their</u> removing the picture* and *<u>Your</u> laughing like that worries me*), but notwithstanding their objections, the fused participle is entirely grammatical and idiomatic English and there is no reason to avoid it.

games

The names of games that are plural in form, such as *billiards*, *bowls*, *darts*, *dominoes*, *draughts* (and the American *checkers*), *skittles*, *snakes and ladders*, etc. are treated as singular nouns in English: *Dominoes is an easy game*. Of course, when the noun refers to the counters, pieces or other items used in these games, it is correctly treated as plural: *If you hit the skittles, they fall over*.

gaol, jail

Both forms of this word are correct in British English, but **jail** is now by far the commoner, **gaol** being in general use only in legal and official contexts. **Jail** is the normal form in all contexts in American English.

If you do choose to use the word **gaol**, be careful to spell it correctly: it is all too easy to write **goal**, with ludicrous results.

Note that **gaol** is pronounced [*jāl*].

gas

The plural of **gas** is **gases**, not **gasses*.

ghastly, gherkin, ghetto, ghost
Do not forget the *h* in these words.

gipsy, gypsy
Both forms are correct but the latter is the commoner.

going to, about to
The phrase **about to** is used when referring to an event expected in the near future: *The train is about to arrive* (= it is expected any minute); *The concert is just about to start*. **Going to** also may be used to refer to events in the immediate future, as in *You can't leave now, the concert is just going to start*, but it is more often used for future events (whether of the close future or not) when what is to be conveyed is an intention to do something, an expectation that something will happen, or the idea that what will happen is the consequence or result of a previous state or present condition, as in *I'm going to retire when I'm sixty* (= intention); *I think it's going to rain* (= expectation); *Are you ever going to get married?* (= intention); *I'm going to have a baby* (= consequence of present state of pregnancy).

good
The adjective **good** is followed by **at** when it means 'clever, skilful', as in *He's very good at putting up shelves*; *I wasn't very good at English at school*. **Good for** means 'beneficial or helpful to', 'suitable for', or 'able to prevent or cure', as in *Cheese is good for you*; *He would be a good man for that job*; *Do you know of anything that is good for warts?* When **good** means 'good at looking after', it is followed by **with**, as in *He is very good with children/horses*.

got
The use of **have got** for **have**, as in *I've got a sore head* and *I've got to finish this essay this evening*, is entirely acceptable in informal English and acceptable to many people in formal contexts as well, though felt to be rather more informal than **have** alone. In written formal English, it is best to use **have** rather than **have got**.

grand-, great-
The prefixes **grand-** and **great-** are used to form compound nouns denoting certain family relationships. **Grand-** is added to **father**, **mother**, **son** and **daughter** and to certain colloquial words for **father** and **mother** such as **pa** and **ma**: *He is my grandfather/grandpa*; *She is my granddaughter*. Both **grand-** and **great-** are used with **aunt**, **uncle**, **nephew**, and **niece**, but the forms with **great-** are commoner than those with **grand-**. **Great-**

alone may be prefixed to words which themselves begin with **grand-** or **great-**: *She is my great-grandmother*, <u>not</u> **grand-grandmother.*

great see **big.**

group terms

Few, if indeed any, speakers of English use the highly specialized terms for groups of particular types of birds and animals such as a *charm* of humming-birds, an *unkindness* of ravens or a *crash* of rhinoceroses. Such terms are found in dictionaries and glossaries and probably nowhere else. There are, however, a number of commonly used words denoting groups of certain species or types of birds and animals, and care must be taken to use the appropriate one. One should speak of a *flock* of birds (but a *covey* of partridges or grouse); a *flock* of sheep or camels; a *herd* of cows, buffaloes, antelopes, horses, and similar animals; a *pack* of dogs or wolves; a *pride* of lions; a *school* or *shoal* of fish (but only a *school* of whales); a *swarm* of bees or flies; a *troop* of monkeys.

guarantee

Note the *u* between the *g* and the *a.*

guerrilla

Note the *u*, the double *r* and the double *l*. A spelling with a single *r* is less common but also correct.

gypsy see **gipsy.**

had, have

An error often heard in speech and not unknown in writing is the insertion of an extra **have** after **had** in conditional constructions such as **If he had have done it, I would have been very angry.* The extra **have** is particularly frequent when it or the preceding **had** is in an abbreviated form: **If he'd have done it, . . .; If he had've done it, ...* Such constructions are quite ungrammatical, and must be avoided: **had** on its own is all that is needed, as in *If he had done it, ...*

haemorrhage

Watch the spelling of this word: note the *ae*, *rr*, and *h.*

half

When **half** refers to a noun or pronoun denoting a single thing or an amount, it is followed by a singular verb: *Half the street has been dug up; Half the sugar is gone; Half a pound of sugar is all we need.*

When **half** refers to a plural noun or pronoun or one denoting a number of individuals, it is followed by a plural verb: *Half of the students are girls*; *About half a dozen children were playing in the street.*

Before a pronoun, **half** must be followed by **of**: *Half of them are girls.* Before a noun, **of** is generally optional (*half the students* and *half of the students* are both correct), but **of** is not used in phrases denoting quantities or times such as *half a dozen, half an hour, half a pound, half a ton.*

hangar

Note the spelling of this word: aeroplanes are kept in **hangars**, clothes are hung up on **hangers**.

hanged, hung

The normal past tense and past participle of the verb **hang** is **hung**: *He hung his clothes in the wardrobe*; *The pictures were hung on the wall.* When the verb refers to suicide, capital punishment, etc., the correct past tense and part participle form is **hanged**: *He hanged himself in a fit of depression.*

harass

Note the spelling – one *r*, two *s*'s.

help, help to

When the verb **help** is followed by another verb, it is not always necessary for the second verb to be preceded by **to**: *Will you help me look for my glasses?* and *Will you help me to look for my glasses?* are both correct. It is never incorrect to insert **to** in such constructions but sometimes wrong to omit it, the rule being that **to** may only be omitted when the subject of the verb **help** is directly and actively involved in the action of the verb which follows. In *Will you help me look for my glasses,* the person addressed as 'you' is being invited to participate actively in the looking, and **to** may therefore be correctly omitted; in *This book helped me to understand the theory of relativity,* the book is not directly participating in my understanding of the theory, and **to** must therefore not be omitted.

here/there is, here/there are

Here and **there** should normally be followed by a singular verb when they are linked to a singular noun phrase or pronoun, and by a plural verb when linked to a plural noun phrase or pronoun: *Here is John now*; *Here are John and Mary*; *There they are*; *There were forty people in the room.* Occasionally, in informal speech, a single verb is used when the noun phrase or pronoun is in the plural, as in **There's the books you need,* but this is not correct and should be avoided.

However, when a plural noun is thought of as denoting a single amount or unit, or a plural noun phrase consists of a series of singular nouns considered separately and successively, a singular verb is correct: *There is fifty pence in that bag* (compare *There are fifty coins in that bag*); *Who could we invite? Well, there's John and Peter and Mike and Sam for a start.*

hiccup, hiccough

The spelling **hiccough** is due to a confusion with **cough**, although the word is pronounced [*hik'up*]. The form **hiccup** is much to be preferred.

high see tall.

historic, historical

These words are not synonyms. **Historic** means 'famous or important in history': *a historic battle; On this historic spot, a battle was fought which changed the course of history.* **Historical** means 'of or about history or people and events from history' (as in *a historical novel; He is engaged in historical research*) or 'having actually happened, or lived as opposed to existing only in legend or fiction' (as in *Is Macbeth a historical person?; Is his murder a historical event/ fact?*).

hoard, horde

Do not confuse these words. A **hoard** is a store or hidden stock of something. A **horde** is a crowd or large number of people, etc.: *Hordes of tourists come here every year.*

hopefully

The use of **hopefully** to mean 'I hope, it is hoped' is sometimes condemned or deprecated, but there is no good reason why this use of the word should not be accepted, and it seems now to be generally acceptable to most speakers of English in informal contexts at least. There is no reason not to use **hopefully** in this sense in formal contexts also, but be prepared for severe criticism from purists if you do so.

horde see hoard.

hospitable

It is correct to stress either the first or the second syllable of this word. The pronunciation with stress on the first syllable is the commoner.

hyphen

For many people, hyphenation is one of the greatest headache-creating aspects of English spelling. However, although there are certain word-types – in particular, compound nouns – in which hyphenation does not seem to follow any logical or consistent rule, there are many categories of word in which the rules are fairly clear-cut and consistent, if not entirely so, and therefore quite simple to follow.

In general, a hyphen is used to show that two or more words are to be treated as a single unit: *She is my mother-in-law*; *a good-looking, hard-working boy*. In many cases, a hyphen is so used to avoid ambiguities: compare *a little-known writer* and *a little, known writer*; *200-odd people* and *200 odd people*. The following are the most important rules of hyphenation:

1. A compound adjective consisting of two words, the second of which is a present or past participle or a word ending in *-ed*, is normally hyphenated: *good-natured*; *black-headed*; *hard-wearing*; *hard-hearted*; *never-ending*; *card-carrying*; *battle-scarred*; *panic-stricken*.

When the first word of such a compound is one of the adverbs **well**, **better**, **best**, **ill**, **worse**, **worst**, a hyphen is inserted only when the compound adjective precedes a noun, not when it occupies other positions in the sentence: *a well-known author* but *He is well known as an author* and *Well known as an author, Jim Brown is now making a name for himself as an actor*.

A past or present participle preceded by an adverb ending in *-ly* is not linked to the adverb by a hyphen in any position in the sentence: *The room is beautifully decorated; a beautifully decorated room*. This rule may be broken if a hyphen is needed for the sake of clarity.

2. Nouns formed from phrasal verbs (i.e. a verb plus *in*, *out*, *off*, etc.) are generally hyphenated: *take-over*; *fly-past*; *shake-up*; *share-out*; *going-over*; *passer-by*. A hyphen should not be used to join the parts of a phrasal verb itself: *We will have to share out the money*, not ...**share-out the money*. Notice the difference between *His going-over* (noun) *of the accounts was very thorough* and *His going over* (verb plus preposition) *the accounts caused a lot of problems*.

3. Phrases of various types, when used as adjectives and preceding the noun they qualify, require hyphens: *an up-to-date report*; *a balance-of-payments problem*; *our next-door neighbours*; *a never-to-be-forgotten experience*.

4. Numbers from 21 to 99 and fractions should be hyphenated: *twenty-three*; *fifty-six*; *one-third*.

5.   Compound adjectives consisting of two simple adjectives or a noun plus an adjective are usually hyphenated when preceding a noun and often (but not always) hyphenated in other positions (e.g. after the verb *be*): *a pitch-dark night; blood-red wine; It's pitch-dark outside.*

6.   In the case of compound nouns, a comparison of the entries in two or more dictionaries will show that there are many words in which hyphenation usage is not clearly established: *coal gas* or *coal-gas; fire-guard* or *fireguard*. In general, a compound noun is written as two words if it is felt that the first word simply qualifies the second word like an adjective, but as a hyphenated word or a single word with no hyphen if the compound is felt to be a single lexical item denoting a particular thing or type of thing: *a bus company, trade figures* but *bus-driver, trademark*. If the 'single lexical item' type of word is well established and frequently used, and is built up from short, one-syllable words, it is likely to be written as a single word with no hyphen: *bedroom; bloodbath; teacup*. A hyphen is more likely in longer words, and where the absence of a hyphen would allow an undesirable or confusing juxtaposition of sounds or letters: *heart-throb* rather than *heartthrob; pole-axe* rather than *poleaxe, time-exposure* rather than **timeexposure.*

7.   Prefixes like *un-*, *dis-*, *mis-*, *re-*, and suffixes like *-fold*, *-ish*, *-most*, *-ness*, *-ship* and *-wise*, are not normally followed, or preceded, by a hyphen. However, if the word to which a prefix is added begins with a capital letter, a hyphen is inserted: *un-English*. Note the use of a hyphen to distinguish *re-cover* (to cover again) from *recover* (to become well again), *re-count* (to count again) from *recount* (to tell), and so on, and to avoid the juxtaposition of two *e*'s in *re-enter*, *re-elect*, etc. *Ex-*, *non-*, and *self-* are normally followed by a hyphen: *ex-wife; non-inflammable; self-respect.*

Hyphens are used to mark breaks in words not normally hyphenated, either when only part of the word is written, as in *four- or fivefold,* (where *four-* represents 'fourfold'), or at the end of a line of writing where part of the word has to be taken over to the next line. In the latter circumstance, the following rules apply:

1.   If possible, split the word into logical parts in such a way that the former part suggests the whole word, or at least does not mislead the reader by suggesting the wrong word: *mis-/shapen* not **miss-/hapen* or **misshap-/en; re-/install,* not **rein-/stall; heat-/ing* not **he-/ating.*

2.   A letter that influences the pronunciation of another letter should not be separated from it at a line-break: *spe-/cial* not **spec-/ial*; *magi-/cian* not **magic-/ian*.

I after a preposition see **me.**

-ible see **-able.**

-ic, -ical, -ically
Many of the adjectives which end in **-ic** and **-ical** are interchangeable. Some are not: see for example the entries at **economic**, **historic**, and **politic**.
Adverbs formed from **-ic/-ical** adjectives almost always end in **-ically:** *frantic, frantically*; *poetic, poetically*. One important exception is *publicly*. For the difference between *politicly* and *politically*, see the entry **politic, political**.

-ics
When a noun ending in **-ics** denotes a science, discipline, or sport, the noun is treated as singular: *Linguistics is the scientific study of language*; *Mathematics is his poorest subject*. When an **-ics** noun denotes a condition, quality, activity, etc., it is treated as plural: *The acoustics in this hall are atrocious*; *Their tactics were to make sudden attacks on the enemy and then disappear into the forest*.

if
In certain constructions, **if** is ambiguous. For example, does the sentence *Let me know if you are coming to the party* mean 'Let me know whether you are coming' or 'Let me know once you have decided to come'? Similarly, does *This is a most enjoyable book, if only occasionally read* mean that the book is enjoyable only if it is only read from time to time, or enjoyable although only read from time to time? The use of **if** in such constructions is grammatically correct, but if it leads to ambiguities, **whether** and **though** are better.
See also **subjunctive.**

illegible, unreadable
Illegible refers to the quality of writing or printing, and means 'impossible to decipher': *illegible handwriting*. **Unreadable** refers to the style, content, etc. of the written or printed material, or to its legibility, and means 'too difficult or boring to read': *His article was so full of jargon, it was quite unreadable*; *His handwriting was so faint, it was unreadable*.

illusion see **delusion.**

imminent see **eminent**.

immoral, amoral

   Immoral means 'wrong', 'wicked', 'not conforming to what are considered correct moral standards'. **Amoral** means 'not concerned with questions of right and wrong', 'not accepting that there are any moral standards by which actions may be judged': *An amoral person may behave in a way considered immoral by other people.*

immunity, impunity

   These words are sometimes confused. **Immunity** means 'freedom (from)' or 'resistance (to)', as in *immunity to measles; Foreign diplomats enjoy diplomatic immunity, which means that they cannot be prosecuted for committing a crime.* **Impunity** refers specifically to 'freedom from punishment or other unpleasant consequences', as in *You cannot expect to break the law with impunity.*

impel see **compel**.

imperial, imperious

   Imperial means 'of an empire or emperor'. **Imperious** means 'proud and overbearing', 'behaving as if expecting to be, or in the habit of being, obeyed': *She disliked his imperious manner.*

impious

   Note the pronunciation of this word: [*im'pi-əs*], not *[*im-pī'əs*].

imply see **infer**.

impracticable, impractical

   Impracticable means 'that cannot be carried out or put into practice': *a completely impracticable idea.* When referring to suggestions, plans, etc., **impractical** (or **unpractical**) means 'possible to carry out but not sensible or convenient'; when referring to people, it means 'not able to do or make things in a sensible and efficient way'.

impunity see **immunity**.

in-, un-

   There is unfortunately no absolutely infallible rule which can be followed to allow one to choose correctly between **un-** or **in-** in forming negative nouns and adjectives, but there are a few guidelines which are often found helpful:

   1. **In-** is added to words which end in suffixes of Latin origin

such as *-ible, -uble, -ence, -ent, -ity, -ice* and *-tude*: *inedible, insolu-ble, incoherence, indecent, insanity, injustice, ingratitude*. **In-** is replaced by **il-** before *l*, **im-** before *b, p, m*, and **ir-** before *r*: *illegible, immobile, impatient, irreverent*. (Note also that the opposite of *noble* is *ignoble*.)

2. **Un-** is added to words ending in *-ed* and *-ing*: *undefeated, unbending*, etc. (three common exceptions being *incapacitated, indisposed* and *inexperienced*).

There are a few words which may take either **in-** or **un-**: *practical, impractical* or *unpractical*. In some cases the **in-** and **un-** forms differ in meaning: *immoral* means 'offending against accepted moral standards', *unmoral* means 'having nothing to do with morality'.

Note that a few words form a negative with **dis-**, e.g. *discourteous, disloyal*, and some with **non-**, e.g. *non-resident, non-inflammable*.

in, at

Both of these prepositions are used in specifying the position or whereabouts of a person, thing, event, etc., the difference being that **in** is used when the idea being conveyed is that of being somewhere within the boundaries of a given area, while **at** is correctly used when one is indicating an exact position. The following examples may help to clarify the rule:

I live in Scotland/in Edinburgh/in George Street (i.e. somewhere within the boundaries of Scotland, Edinburgh, George Street), but *I live at 12 George Street, Edinburgh* (my exact address).

I am standing in George Street (somewhere in the street) but *I am standing at the corner of George Street and Castle Street* (exact position).

I live in Edinburgh (a large city) but *I live at* or *in Juniper Green* (both **at** and **in** are allowed with small villages, suburbs, etc., because they can be thought of as being small enough to allow the **at** which indicates a specific position or as being large enough to allow the **in** which indicates position within an area). Similarly the use of **at** rather than **in** in *The plane refuelled at Edinburgh* indicates that Edinburgh is here being thought of as a point on the map, a specific place on a journey.

The same 'specific/non-specific' distinction between **at** and **in** applies also to their use with buildings:

When a type of building or place of work is referred to, **in** is used, but when a particular place is referred to it should be preceded by **at**: *I work in a factory/office/shop*, but *I work at Smiths* *the Grocers* (**in** is allowable with large stores); *I work in a hotel* but *I work at the Grand Hotel.*

Note also *at home* but *in the house*, *at school* (attending school) and *in school* (actually in the school).

include see **comprise.**

incredible, incredulous

Incredible means 'unbelievable'; **incredulous** means 'not believing, showing disbelief'. If you are told an *incredible* story, you may become *incredulous*, and show your *incredulity* at the *incredibility* of the tale.

index

The normal plural of **index** is **indexes**. The plural form **indices** is now used only in technical senses, e.g. in mathematics.

indict

Note the pronunciation of this legal term: [*in-dīt'*].

indoor, indoors

Indoors is an adverb meaning 'in or into the house': *Stay indoors*; *She turned and ran indoors.* **Indoor** is an adjective: *indoor games.*

infectious, contagious

An **infectious** disease is one which is spread through the air, etc. by germs. A **contagious** disease is one which is spread by direct physical contact with a person suffering from the disease or by contact with something which has itself been in direct contact with such a person. When **infectious** and **contagious** are used figuratively, there is no difference in meaning: laughter, for example, can be **contagious** or **infectious**.

infer, imply

Strictly speaking, **infer** means 'to form an opinion by reasoning from what one knows', as in *I inferred from your silence that you were angry*, and **imply** means 'to suggest or hint at (something) without actually stating it', as in *Are you implying that I'm a liar?* **Infer** is often used nowadays in the sense of **imply**, but although acceptable to many people in informal speech and writing, this use is best avoided in formal contexts.

inferior

The adjective **inferior**, meaning 'not as good or important as', behaves like a comparative adjective but must be followed by **to**, not *∗**than**: *This book is inferior to that one.*

inflammable see **flammable**.

inflict see **afflict**.

ingenious, ingenuous

> **Ingenious** means 'clever, skilful' or 'cleverly made or thought out': *an ingenious plan*. **Ingenuous** means 'frank, trusting, not cunning or deceitful': *It was rather ingenuous of you to believe a liar like him*.

inquire see **enquire**.

insure, ensure, assure

> These three words are sometimes confused. To **insure** someone or something is to arrange for the payment of a sum of money in the event of loss, accident or injury: *He insured his life for £20 000*. To **ensure** is a rather formal word for 'to make sure': *You should ensure that your television set is switched off at night*. To **assure** means 'to state positively' as in *I assured him that the house was empty* or, in rather formal usage, 'to make (someone) sure' as in *You may wish first to assure yourself of his honest intentions*. **Assure** is now only rarely used in the sense of **insure** given above.
>
> **Assurance** means 'confidence', as in *I envy him his assurance* and *self-assurance*, or 'a promise' as in *He gave me his assurance that he would help*. In the sense of 'insurance', **assurance** is now becoming rare: one may speak of *life assurance* or *life insurance*, but in general, **insurance** is the commoner term.

intense, intensive

> **Intense** means 'very great': *intense heat*; *a feeling of intense bitterness*. **Intensive** means 'concentrated, thorough, taking great care': *an intensive search*; *the intensive care ward of a hospital*.

into, in to

> **Into** is a preposition indicating movement from outside something to a position on the inside, as in *He walked into the room*, movement against something, as in *The car ran into a lamp-post*, or a change of state or condition, as in *The wizard turned them into frogs*. **In to** consists of an adverb **in** and a preposition **to**, and must not be confused with **into**. Distinguish for example between *He came into the room*, *He came in to tell us what had happened* and *He escorted her in to dinner* (i.e. into the room in order to have dinner, not actually into the dinner itself).

inversion of subject and verb

> The subject of a verb normally precedes the verb in statements in

English and follows it in questions: *John arrived*; *I am John Smith*; *Did John arrive?*; *Are you John Smith?* There are, however, certain contexts in which the subject of a verb in a statement may follow the verb:

1. After *here* and *there*, a noun or noun phrase follows the verb: *Here comes John*; *There stood the man I had been looking for*. With a pronoun there is no inversion: *There they are*.

2. After certain negative words or words with a negative implication standing at the beginning of a clause, there is inversion: *Scarcely had he arrived when he was asked to leave again*; *Never had I been so embarrassed as on that day*; *Little does he know that I have guessed his secret*; *Not only was he rude to the teacher, he also hit the headmaster*. Similarly after *nor*: *He was neither clever, nor was he very brave*.

3. There is inversion in a conditional clause without *if*: *Had I known that, I would not have come* (= if I had known that, . . .).

4. There is inversion after *so* which is linked to a following *that*, as in *So often did he fall over on the ice that in the end he stopped trying to skate*.

5. Inversion can be used for dramatic effect, emphasis, etc., as in *Down came the rain*. As with *here* and *there*, there is no inversion with pronoun subjects: *Off he went*.

inverted commas see **quotation marks**.

-ise, -ize

Many verbs in English may be spelt with **-ise** or **-ize**, e.g. *equalise/equalize*; *terrorise/terrorize*. There are some, however, which must always be spelt **-ise**, e.g. *advertise*, *despise*, *televise*. The problem is to remember which group a particular verb belongs to. The following guidelines may be of some help:

1. If the final syllable of the verb is not pronounced [*īz*], it will be written with an *s*: *promise*, *braise*, *raise*.

2. If the **-ise** is part of the root of the verb rather than a suffix added to the root, it will be written with an *s*: *advise*, *arise*, *comprise*, *despise*, *disguise*, *incise*, *revise*, *rise*, *supervise*, *surprise*, etc. Words ending in *-cise*, *-mise*, *-prise* and *-vise* are very likely to belong to this group if what precedes the *-ise* is not recognizable as an English word: there is, for example, no word *desp or *superv in English. Note however that *capsize* is always written with a *z*, never an *s*.

3. If the **-ise** is added to a word or word-root as a suffix, it may

also be written **-ize**: *critic*, *criticise/criticize*; *item*, *itemise/itemize*; *modern*, *modernise/modernize*; *victim*, *victimise/victimize*; *oxide*, *oxidise/oxidize*; *sympathy*, *sympathise/sympathize*. Note however that *advertise*, which looks like a verb of this category, cannot be written *advertize, and *antagonise*, *baptise*, *ostracise* and *recognise*, which do not look as if they belong to this group, may be spelt *antagonize*, *baptize*, etc.

4. Words spelt with a *y* are always spelt with an *s* in British English: *analyse*, *paralyse*. In American English, they are spelt with *z*.

its, it's

Its is the possessive form of **it**: *The dog buried its bone*. **It's** means 'it is' or 'it has': *It's going to rain*; *It's got to stop raining sometime*.

-ize see -ise.

jail see gaol.

jewellery, jewelry

Both spellings are acceptable, but the former is more common in British English, the latter in American English.

judgement, judgment

Both spellings are acceptable, but the first variant is the more common.

judicial, judicious

Judicial is a formal word meaning 'pertaining to judges and law-courts'. **Judicious** means 'showing wisdom and good sense': *a judicious choice of words*.

kerb, curb

A **kerb**, in British English, is the edging of a pavement. A **curb** is something which holds back, restrains, or controls: *We'll have to put a curb on his wild enthusiasm*. **Curb** may also be used as a verb: *Curb your enthusiasm*.

In American English, **curb** is the usual spelling for all the above senses.

kilometre

The preferred pronunciation of this word is [kil'ō-mē-tər], but [kil-om'i-tər] is also accepted.

kind of

In informal speech and writing, **kind of** is usually preceded by *these* or *those* rather than *this* or *that* when what follows is a plural noun: *those kind of people*; *these kind of flowers*. Although strictly speaking ungrammatical, such constructions are quite acceptable in informal language, but they must not be used in formal contexts. Constructions with the singular adjectives *this* and *that* followed by a plural noun (e.g. *this kind of flowers*) often sound awkward or pedantic, so in formal speech and writing the only thing one can do is rephrase the expression, and say *this kind of flower* with a singular noun or *flowers of this kind* with the plural noun at the head of the phrase.

The same applies to **sort of**.

knit

The past tense and past participle of the verb **knit** may be either **knitted** or **knit**. **Knitted** is the normal form when the verb denotes the making of garments, etc. with knitting-needles and wool: *She knitted a pair of socks*; *a knitted hat*. **Knit** is the form generally used in other contexts, as in *Their dependence on one another knit them into a close group*, but when the verb is linked with the noun *brows*, **knitted** is also possible: *He knit/knitted his brows as he read the letter* (= He frowned, wrinkled his brows).

knowledgeable

Watch the spelling of this word: do not forget the *e* before the *a*.

large see big.

latter see former.

lay, lie

These words are very frequently confused. **Lay** means 'to place in a flat, prone or horizontal position'. It is a transitive verb, which requires an object. The present tense forms are **lay**, **lays**, the present participle **laying**, the past tense **laid** and the past participle **laid**: *If you lay the pen down there, it will roll off the table*; *I'm sure I laid it here yesterday*. **Lie** means 'to be or move into a flat, prone or horizontal position'. It is an intransitive verb, which does not have an object. The present tense forms are **lie**, **lies**, the present participle **lying**, the past tense **lay**, the past participle **lain**: *She went into the bedroom and lay on the bed*.

In the sense of 'to tell lies', the past tense and past participle of **lie** are **lied** and **lied**: *He lied to me yesterday*; *He has often lied to me*.

lend, loan

Lend is always a verb: *Can you lend me £5?* **Loan** may be used as a noun or a verb: *a loan of £5*; *Can you loan me £5?* The use of **loan** as a verb is more common in American English than in British English, and many speakers still prefer to use **lend** rather than **loan** as the verb form, but both are accepted by the best authorities.

lengthy see **long**.

less see **fewer**.

liable, apt, likely, prone

These four adjectives may all be used to indicate a probability, natural inclination, or tendency, but although very similar in meaning, they are not synonymous, and care should be taken to use the adjective which best conveys the meaning you intend.

Liable and **apt**, in particular, are frequently confused, the one being used where the other would be more appropriate. **Apt** should be used to convey the idea that a person or thing has a tendency to do something or is in the habit of doing something, as in *She is apt to ask silly questions* or *Nails as thin as that are apt to break*. **Liable**, on the other hand, conveys not only the idea that something will probably happen or generally happens, but moreover that what will or does happen is unpleasant or undesirable, and usually, but not always, that it is a consequence of some previous action or event: *Children who play with pins are liable to prick themselves*; *If she drinks too much wine, she is liable to say something silly.*

Likely is correctly used when one is referring to the probability of something happening at a particular time or place or in a particular set of circumstances: *If you don't hurry up, you are likely to miss the bus*; *You had better take an umbrella, it's likely to rain this afternoon.*

Prone is close in meaning to **apt**, but should only be used of people or of nouns denoting things in which people are involved, such as *factory, industry,* etc. **Prone** is more appropriate than **apt** when one is referring to bad or unpleasant aspects of a person's disposition or personality, as in *She is prone to lose her temper* or *She is prone to tantrums*, or to the tendency for unpleasant or unfortunate things (such as illness or accidents) to happen to a person, as in *She is prone to catch colds*; *She is prone to colds*.

Apt to, **liable to** and **likely to** can only be followed by an infinitive: *apt to break*; *liable to break*; *likely to break*. **Prone to**, on the other hand, may equally correctly be followed by a noun, an infinitive or a verb ending in **-ing**: *She is prone to accidents*; *He is prone to dream in school*; *He is prone to dreaming in school*. **Prone** is also frequently used to form compound adjectives, such as *accident-prone*.

libel, slander

The essential difference between these two terms is that **libel** is an untrue defamatory statement made in a permanent form such as print, writing or pictures or broadcast on radio or television, whereas **slander** is one made by means of the spoken word (not broadcast) or gesture.

licence, license see -ce, -se.

lie see lay.

lieutenant

Note the spelling of this word, especially the *ieu*. The pronunciation of **lieutenant** varies according to context: the general pronunciation in British English is [*lef-ten'ənt*]; in the navy the word was formerly always, and sometimes still is, pronounced [*lə-ten'ənt*]; in American English, the pronunciation is [*l$\overline{oo}$-ten'ənt*].

lighted, lit

Both forms are possible for the past tense and past participle of the verb **light**, but **lit** is more common in verbal use, **lighted** when the past participle is being used as an adjective: *She lit the fire*; *a lighted match*.

lightning

Note that the **lightning** which often accompanies thunder has no *e* in it, unlike the present participle of the verb **lighten**.

like, as

There are certain constructions in English involving the notion of comparison, in which **like** and **as** (or **as if**) are sometimes confused or misused. The following general rules apply in such cases:

1. When making comparisons of any sort, **like** should be used when what follows is a noun, noun-phrase, or pronoun: *He talks like his father*; *It looks like a stone*; *He writes like an expert on the subject*.

2. When comparisons are made between actions, events, etc., and what follows is a clause (i.e. a construction which includes a verb) rather than a noun or pronoun, **like** is generally used in informal contexts: *I just can't sing like I used to*; *Do like I do*. In formal speech and writing, many people prefer **as** to **like** in such constructions e.g. *Do as I do*, but **like** is also widely accepted, and is found in the works of some of the best

English writers. If a rough generalization and distinction can be made, **like** is often preferred when a real comparison is being made between the way in which things are done, **as** when one is commenting on the fact of something being done again, when one is giving an example to follow, or the like (i.e. when no actual comparison is involved): compare, for example, *She sings just like her mother did* (= in the same way as her mother) and *She sings just as her mother did* (i.e. her mother sang and she does too). However, it must not be thought that this is a hard-and-fast rule: the use of **as** or **like** in constructions like this is variable.

If the comparison is being made to some hypothetical or possible event, **like** is acceptable only in the most informal speech, and it is generally preferable to use **as if**: *It looks like we might win after all* (informal); *It looks as if we might win after all*; *He was running as if all the devils in hell were after him.*

Note the difference between *I feel like I'm dancing* (= I feel as if I am dancing) and *I feel like dancing* (= I want to dance).

3. Like **like**, **as** may be followed in some constructions by a noun or noun-phrase: *I am speaking to you now as a friend.* The difference between **as** and **like** in such constructions is that **as** is used when the person, etc. actually has the role or status defined by what follows the preposition, whereas **like** is used when he, etc. is simply behaving as if he had such a role or status. Some examples may clarify this distinction: *He treats me like a child* (i.e. I do not think I am a child but he treats me as if I were); *You are a child and I shall treat you as a child*; *He treats me not just as a son but as a friend* (i.e. I am his son and he also considers me to be his friend). However, **like** is not infrequently found where **as** would, according to the above rules, be expected: *You are a child and I shall treat you like a child.*

Notice that **like** and **as**, when used as prepositions, should be followed by **me**, **him**, etc. rather than **I**, **he**, etc.: *He sings like me*, not * *He sings like I.*

Care must be taken with **like** and **as** to ensure that the comparison that is made actually compares the things that were intended to be compared. In the sentence * *Like me, my brother's hatred of nuclear weapons is intense*, what is actually linked up by **like** is 'me' and 'hatred', although it is clearly 'me' and 'my brother' that are being compared; the sentence needs to be rephrased, e.g. *Like me, my brother has an intense hatred of nuclear weapons.*

likely see **liable.**

liquefy

Note the spelling of this word, which is often spelt *liquify*, a spelling no doubt due to the influence of *liquid*.

lit see **lighted**.

literally

Do not use **literally** unless you literally mean 'literally', i.e. 'exactly what is meant by the following or preceding words'. A statement such as *I had had nothing to eat since lunchtime so I was literally starving* is clearly not meant to be taken literally at all. Use **literally** only if you wish to emphasize that what is being said is to be understood in a straightforward literal way (e.g. *Because of the drought, many people in Africa are literally starving*).

little, a little

Like **few** and **a few**, **little** and **a little** differ in that they emphasize the negative and positive side of a situation respectively: *There is little bread left* means 'There is not much bread left'; *There is a little bread left* emphasizes that there is nonetheless some bread left.

little, small

Like their opposites **big**, **large**, and **great**, the adjectives **little** and **small** are interchangeable in some contexts but not in others.

Little and **small** are both used in referring to physical size: *a little book, a small book; a little dog, a small dog.* **Little** rather than **small** is used when smallness due to age is implied: *Don't blame him, he is only a little boy* (i.e. not very old). **Small** is generally used when smallness in terms of importance is meant: *a small business; I'd like to clarify a few small points;* **little** is occasionally used in this sense: *There are a couple of little details that I'd like to clarify.*

When referring to physical quantities, **small** is used: *Only a small number of people turned up; Add a small amount of salt.* When referring to quantity or duration with abstract nouns, **little** is preferred: *It makes very little noise; It would take little time to finish this; We have little hope of doing that.* **Small** is also used in this sense in certain phrases such as *small thanks, small wonder, small consolation, small reason,* but with these nouns too **little** is quite correct.

loan see **lend**.

long, lengthy

Long is the normal adjective for describing things of great length. **Lengthy** is generally applied only to speech or writing (*e.g. a lengthy speech; a lengthy essay*) and often has an implication of something being too long or tediously long.

luggage

Like **baggage**, **luggage** is a singular collective noun: *My luggage consists of three suitcases.* For many, but not all, speakers of British English, **luggage** is the normal term for suitcases, etc. carried on a journey on land, but **baggage** if the journey is by sea or air. **Baggage** is the normal term in all contexts in American English.

lunch, luncheon, dinner

Dinner is the main meal of the day, usually including a course of meat and vegetables, and often soup, a dessert, etc. It may be eaten either in the middle of the day or in the evening. **Dinner** is also used of a formal evening gathering at which such a meal (usually of several courses) is served.

Lunch is the term for a meal eaten in the middle of the day, whether a snack or a more substantial meal. **Luncheon** is a formal term for **lunch**, used only in set expressions like *luncheon voucher* and *luncheon-meat* and when referring to a formal midday gathering at which a meal is served: *A luncheon was held in his honour.*

luxuriant, luxurious

These very similar adjectives are frequently confused. **Luxuriant** has nothing to do with luxury but means 'abundant, prolific, growing vigorously', as in *the luxuriant growth of jungle plants*; *a luxuriant moustache.* **Luxurious** means 'pertaining to luxury and riches, expensive' as in *a luxurious house.*

mad

In colloquial English, **mad** may mean 'angry' or 'having a great liking or desire'. In the latter sense it is followed by **about**: *He's mad about cars/the girl next door.* In the sense of 'angry', it is followed by **at** or **with** when referring to a person, **at** or **about** when referring to a thing, happening, etc.: *He was mad at/with me for forgetting my key*; *I got really mad at the suggestion that you had cheated* ; *I'm really mad about that* (**at** being preferred when a sudden feeling of anger is implied, **about** when the anger is felt sometime after the event causing it; compare the comments at **angry**).

In the sense of 'acting wildly, (as if) out of one's mind', **mad** is followed by **with** when referring to the cause of the madness: *He was going mad with thirst.*

madam, madame

The normal form of this word in English is **madam**, pronounced [ma'dəm], often written with a capital. It is used as a polite term of respect, as in *I will see if I can find the coat you are looking for, madam*, and is sometimes used before the title of a lady's official position when she is being addressed formally, as in *Madam Chairman*.

Madame, pronounced [ma'dəm] or [ma-däm'], is the French equivalent of **Mrs**, and is correctly used instead of **Mrs** when referring to ladies from French-speaking countries.

The plural of **madame** is **mesdames** (pronounced [mā'däm] or [mā-däm']). **Mesdames** is also sometimes used as the plural of **madam**, which has no plural of its own in the sense given above (in other senses, the plural is **madams**).

magic, magical

The adjective **magic** generally means 'pertaining to magic': *a magic wand*; *He rode on a magic carpet*. **Magical**, on the other hand, means 'as if caused by magic, enchanting', as in *It was a magical experience*; *a magical change of character*.

majority

Majority should not be used when referring to things not divisible into separate units or individuals: *the majority of the crowd*; *the majority of the members* but not * *the majority of the cake* or * *the majority of the letter*. With the latter type of noun, use **most of** instead. (**Most of** is also often preferable with the former category of noun as well.)

Phrases containing **majority** may be followed by either singular or plural verbs, pronouns, etc. depending on the sense: *The majority of those present were in favour of the plans* (**majority** thought of as a number of individuals); *The majority of the group was in favour of the plans* (**majority** thought of as a body of people).

male, masculine

The adjective **male** differs from **masculine** in the same way as **female** differs from **feminine**. **Male** means 'of the sex that normally fathers young or has similar sexual characteristics: *A male horse is called a stallion*; *a male flower on a plant*. **Masculine** may only be applied to people (men or women), and means 'characteristic of a man, having the qualities or characteristics one would expect or wish for in a man': *a woman with a rather masculine bearing*.

malign, malignant see **benign**.

manoeuvre

Note the spelling of this often misspelt word, especially the *oeu*. The normal American spelling is **maneuver**.

masculine see **male**.

masterful, masterly

These two adjectives were once synonymous, but are so no longer. **Masterful** means 'showing power, authority, or determination': *Some women like their husbands to be masterful*. **Masterly** means 'showing the skill of a master', and is not applied to people but to their performance or actions: *a masterly display of swordsmanship*. **Masterful** is sometimes used in the sense of **masterly** given here, but the distinction outlined above is best adhered to.

may see **can**.

me *or* **I**

There are two positions in which **me** and **I** are often wrongly substituted one for the other: after the verb **be** and after a preposition.

1. Expressions such as *It's me* and *It was me* are entirely acceptable in modern English. The use of **I** in such expressions sounds over-formal or pompous. However, if the pronoun is linked to a following clause, **I** rather than **me** should be used: *It was I who broke the window*. *It was me who broke the window* would be acceptable only in informal speech.

2. After a preposition, **me** should always be used: *Come with me*. Errors sometimes occur when the object of the preposition is two pronouns linked by **and**, e.g. ** between you and I*, ** like you and I*. Such phrases should of course be *between you and me* and *like you and me*.

The same rules apply to **he** and **him**, **she** and **her**, etc.: *It was she who broke it*; *the skill of us professionals*.

media see **medium**.

mediaeval, medieval

Both forms of this word are correct, but the second form is now the preferred form in British English as it is in American English.

medium

In the sense of 'a person through whom the spirits of the dead are supposed to speak', the plural of this word is **mediums**. In the sense of 'radio, television and newspapers', the plural is **media**:

the news media. In all other senses, both **mediums** and **media** are correct.

Note that **media** (= news media) is sometimes treated as a singular noun. This is not correct. **Media** must always be linked to a plural verb, pronoun, etc.

meet, meet with

In British English, one **meets** a person, but **meets with** approval, misfortune, or opposition. In American English, it is correct to say **meet with** with people also: *They met with the representatives of various companies while they were in Britain.*

meter, metre

Be careful not to confuse these words: **metre** is a unit of measurement, **meter** an instrument for measuring (e.g. *a gas meter*). In American English, both words are spelt **meter**.

middle see **centre**.

million, billion, *etc.*

A **million** is 1 000 000, both in British and American English.

In British English, a **billion** is a million millions, 1 000 000 000 000; in American English, it is a thousand millions, 1 000 000 000. Similarly, a **trillion** is a million billions (1 followed by eighteen zeros) in British English, but a thousand billions (1 followed by twelve zeros) in American English. For each number further up the scale (e.g. **quadrillion**, **quintillion**, **sextillion**, none of which are very common), British usage adds six zeros to the preceding number, American usage adds three.

The situation is further confused by the fact that in scientific and economic contexts, many speakers of British English use **billion** in the American rather than British sense.

Miss

The correct way to refer to two or more ladies whose name is 'Miss Black' is *the Misses Black. The Miss Blacks* is not strictly correct, but is acceptable in informal speech.

mistrust see **distrust**.

misuse see **abuse**.

Mohammedan see **Moslem**.

mongoose

This word is not related to **goose**, and the plural is **mongooses**, not *mongeese.

Moslem, Muslim, Mohammedan

Both **Moslem** and **Muslim** are correct, but the second is now more common than the first. The term **Mohammedan** is not acceptable to many Muslims, and is therefore better avoided altogether lest one cause offense.

Muslim may be pronounced with an [ŏŏ] or an [u] in the first syllable.

much see **very.**

Muslim see **Moslem.**

must see **need.**

mutual see **common.**

naught see **nought.**

need (*noun*)

The noun **need** is followed by the preposition **for**: *There is no need for panic; Was there any need for such secrecy?* However the phrases **have need** and **in need** are followed by **of**: *The car was badly in need of repair.*

need (*verb*)

Like **dare**, the verb **need** may behave either like a full verb (like **walk, sing**, etc.) or like an auxiliary verb (like **can, will, should**, etc.). The full verb **need** is always followed by **to** when it precedes another verb and ends in *-s* in the third person singular of the present tense, whereas the auxiliary verb **need** is not followed by **to** and has no *-s* in the third person singular. The following rules apply:

1. When **need** means 'to require, be in need of', it acts as a full verb: *This page needs to be checked again.* In this sense, **need** may also be followed by a verb form ending in **-ing**: *This page needs checking again.*

2. In the sense of 'to have to, be obliged to', **need** may behave either as a full verb or as an auxiliary verb. In the present tense, only the full verb form is possible with an affirmative statement: *He needs to leave at five o'clock.* Both full verb and auxiliary verb constructions are possible with negative statements and with questions: *He doesn't need to leave; He needn't leave; Does he need to leave?; Need he leave?* In the past tense, only the full verb is possible: *He didn't need to leave; Did he need to leave?* Note the difference between *He didn't need to go* and *He needn't have gone.* The first construction is correct whether or not the person

actually went: *He didn't need to go but he went anyway*; *He didn't need to go so he didn't go*. The second construction is possible only if the person did go: *He needn't have gone, but he went anyway*.

neither

Like **either**, **neither** should be followed by a singular verb: *Neither of them is free*. **Neither** should only be used when referring to one of two people, things, etc.; with larger numbers use **none** or **no**.

Care should be taken to link **neither** with **nor**, never with *or*: *neither one thing nor the other* is correct; *neither one thing or the other* is not.

There is sometimes some uncertainty about the correct verb-form to use with **neither ... nor**. In general, the verb should agree with the noun or pronoun which is closest to it, i.e. the one following **nor**: *Neither you nor I am going*; *Neither you nor Mary is going*; *Neither John nor his friends are going*. However, when the noun or pronoun following **neither** is plural and that following **nor** is singular, most people feel that the use of a singular verb to agree with the second noun sounds awkward or unnatural, and a plural verb is generally preferred: *Neither John's brothers nor his sister are going*.

As with **either ... or**, one must be careful to ensure that the words or phrases which follow **neither** and **nor** match in construction: *I can neither think of a better method nor a cheaper one* would be better as *I can think of neither a better method nor a cheaper one*.

nice

Nice is a very nice word, but there are many other adjectives that can be used to show one's approval. Overuse of **nice** often suggests a lack of care or clarity in thinking.

none

None may be followed by either a singular or a plural verb, whichever is logically appropriate. When denoting a quantity or amount, **none** should be followed by a singular verb: *None of the milk was spilt*. When referring to a plural noun, **none** will be followed by a singular noun if the emphasis is on each individual person or thing of the group denoted by the plural noun, but plural if the emphasis is on all or part of the group as a whole: *None of us have been to France*; *None of them speak French*; *We all had to sing a song or recite a poem — none of us was allowed to say no*.

no one

As a pronoun, both **no one** and **no-one** are correct, but the former is the more common form nowadays.

not

Sentences containing **not** linked with words like **all** and **every** are sometimes ambiguous. For example, does the sentence *All schoolboys don't wear caps nowadays* mean that 'no schoolboy wears a cap' or that 'not every schoolboy wears a cap'? If there is any possibility of ambiguity or doubt about your intended meaning, rephrase the sentence, e.g. *Not all schoolboys wear caps nowadays* or *No schoolboys wear caps nowadays*.

not only ... but also

Like **either ... or** and **neither ... nor**, the construction **not only ... but also** requires correct balance and matching between what follows **not only** and what follows **but also**: **We are not only interested in your book but also in you as a person* would be better rephrased *We are interested not only in your book but also in you as a person*.

nought, naught

Nought and **naught** are in origin one and the same word, the variant spellings matching *bought* and *caught* respectively. However, in present-day English, the two spellings are normally kept separate: **nought** is a zero, the figure 0; **naught** is nothing, usually found in phrases such as *come to naught*, *set at naught*.

number

A number of preceding a plural noun is treated as an adjective phrase, meaning 'some', and is followed by a plural verb: *A number of children were playing in the street*. **The number of** is followed by a singular verb, e.g. *The number of deaths from lung cancer is increasing*, as in such a construction the verb is linked to the singular noun **number** rather than to the plural noun which follows.

O, oh

Oh is the normal form in present-day English: *Oh, what a surprise!*; *Oh, look at that big red balloon!* It is normally followed by a comma or an exclamation mark except in short exclamations like *Oh no!* or *Oh dear!* **O** is now found almost only in poetry, especially when addressing someone or expressing a wish: *O Skylark, bird of heavenly joy!*; *O for the wings of a dove!* It is never separated from the following word by a comma or exclamation mark.

oblivious

Originally, **oblivious** meant 'forgetting, no longer aware', and was followed by the preposition **of**. Now the meaning has widened to 'unaware, unconscious (of)' and in this sense **oblivious** may correctly be followed by **of** or **to**.

observance, observation

Observance and **observation** each correspond to different meanings of the verb **observe**. To **observe** a law is to obey that law, to **observe** a tradition is to follow or comply with that tradition, and the noun corresponding to these senses of **observe** is **observance**: *the observance of the speed limits; the observance of religious holidays*. **Observation** means 'the act of watching or noticing', as in *The police kept the man under observation*, and is also a rather formal word for 'a remark, comment', as in *He made a polite observation about her new dress*.

occur, take place

To **occur** means 'to happen by chance', as in *The accident occurred yesterday morning*. **Take place** means 'to happen as a result of planning', as in *The sports meeting will take place next Monday*.

occurrence

Note the *cc* and *rr* in this word, and in **occurred** and **occurring**.

of, 's

It is impossible to give a concise, hard-and-fast rule governing the choice of **of** and **'s** in the formation of possessive and similar constructions. Indeed, with many nouns both **of** and **'s** are possible: *this car's engine* or *the engine of this car; a bee's wings* or *the wings of a bee*. However, the following guidelines which indicate tendencies rather than rules may be of some assistance:

1. **'s** is very much more common than **of** with nouns denoting or naming people, animals and places: *John's dog; the boy's dog; our party's policies; the dog's tail; Scotland's oil*. With short proper nouns, **'s** is virtually obligatory in a genuine possessive sense: *John's book*, not* *the book of John; of* is acceptable in the sense of 'depicting' (*a statue of John*) or 'directed towards' (*for the love of John*).

2. **'s** is often used with nouns denoting regions, institutions, etc.: *the country's economic development; the town's ratepayers; the earth's core; the school's playing-fields*. **Of** is also possible: *the economic development of the country.*

3. **'s** is usually used with nouns denoting time: *a day's holiday; today's task*.

4. **'s** is more commonly used than **of** with a number of other

nouns denoting parts of the body, means of transport, certain activities and qualities, etc.: *the brain's function*; *the car's tyres*; *life's disappointments*; *the play's first scene*. **Of** is also possible: *the function of the brain*.

5. With most other nouns, **of** rather than **'s** is normal, if not obligatory: *the roof of the house*; *the width of the road*.

official, officious

Official means 'done by someone in authority', 'pertaining to authority', etc.: *the official result of the race*. **Officious** means 'too eager to meddle, offering unwanted advice or assistance'.

oh see **O**.

older see **elder**.

one

Note that the possessive form of the pronoun **one** has an apostrophe (*one's*), unlike *hers*, *its*, etc.

One is correctly used to mean 'people in general', as in *One can sometimes see the coast of France from here*. The use of **one** as a replacement for 'I' is considered affected by most people, and should be avoided: if you mean 'I', say *I*. In British English, if **one** has been used in a sentence, all subsequent pronouns with the same reference must be **one**, **one's**, etc.: *One must look after oneself and one's own property.* In American English, **one** is normally followed by **he**, **him**, etc.: *One must look after himself and his own property*.

A common mistake that occurs in certain sentences with **one** is incorrect agreement between subject and verb (i.e. failure to make the verb agree with its true subject because the structure or meaning of the sentence leads one to make it agree with some other word or words). In **He is one of those people who enjoys gardening*, the verb *enjoys* has been made singular to agree with *he* or *one* whereas it should be the plural form *enjoy* to agree with *those people who*. On the other hand, *I am one who enjoys gardening* is correct as the verb here must be singular to agree with *one who*. A similar mistake can be seen in **One in two of the citizens of this town own a car*, in which the verb has been made plural in agreement with the notional plural subject 'citizens' (i.e. all the citizens who own a car), whereas the true subject of the verb *own* is *one*, and the verb must therefore be singular (as can more easily be seen if one rephrases the sentence slightly: *Of the citizens of this town, one in two owns a car*).

one another see **each other.**

only

Like **even**, **only** must be positioned correctly in a sentence if one is to be certain of conveying the meaning one intends to convey In written English at least, **only** should stand immediately before the word or words in a sentence which it is meant to refer to, as in the following examples:

Only John wrote to me (= John and no-one else).

John only wrote to me (= he did nothing more than write).

John wrote only to me (= to me and to no-one else).

In spoken English, intonation and stress usually help to convey the intended meaning, and there is therefore greater freedom in the positioning of **only**:

John only <u>wrote</u> to me (with the stress on *wrote*) means he did nothing more than write.

John only wrote to <u>me</u> (with stress on *me*) means he wrote to me and to no-one else.

on to, onto

Unlike **into**, **onto** is not a word-form accepted by everyone. Many people still prefer **on to** as two words even in senses corresponding to **into**. However, both **on to** and **onto** must be considered correct prepositional forms in present-day English: *The book fell on to* (or *onto*) *the table.* Of course, when **on to** consists of an adverb and a preposition, it must never be written as a single word: *He went on to tell me about his life in Africa*, not* *He went onto tell me.*

onward, onwards

Onward may be used as an adjective or adverb: *the onward march of time*; *Time marches onward*. **Onwards** may only be used as an adverb, but is less common than **onward**.

-or see **-er.**

oral, aural, verbal

Because of their similarity in sound, **oral** and **aural** are sometimes confused. **Oral** means 'of the mouth', 'taken in by the mouth', 'spoken as opposed to written': *oral hygiene*; *an oral contraceptive*; *an oral exam*. **Aural** means 'pertaining to the ear': *an exercise in aural comprehension.*

The adjective **verbal** is ambiguous. It may mean either 'spoken as opposed to written' or 'in spoken or written words as opposed to gestures, etc.'. In some contexts, the meaning of **verbal** will no doubt be quite clear; in others, it may be necessary to avoid a possible ambiguity either by replacing **verbal** with **oral** or by rephrasing the sentence altogether.

outdoor, outdoors

Outdoor is an adjective, **outdoors** an adverb: *outdoor activities*; *Don't go outdoors if it is raining*. The phrase **out of doors** is also used as an adverb: *We like to eat out of doors on warm summer evenings*.

outward, outwards

As is the case with other words ending in **-ward(s)**, **outward** may be used as both an adjective and an adverb, **outwards** as an adverb only: *He gave no outward sign of his unhappiness*; *The outward journey will be by sea, but they will return by air*; *Moving outwards from the centre of the painting, we see that the figures become smaller*.

Although both **outwards** and **outward** may be used as adverbs, they are not absolutely synonymous: **outwards** is commoner than **outward**, and is used in all contexts where movement, etc. towards the edge or outside of something is meant. **Outward** is used of the direction of a ship sailing from its home port, especially in the phrase *outward bound*, and in figurative rather than literal senses as in the adjective *outward-looking* (= interested in people, places, etc. beyond one's own immediate environment).

over see above.

owing to see because of.

paradigm, paradigmatic

Note that there is a *g* in both these words. It is silent in **paradigm** (pronounced [*pa'rə-dīm*]), but pronounced in **paradigmatic** ([*pa-rə-dig-mat'ik*]).

paraffin

A word often misspelt. Note the single *r* and double *f*.

parallel

Another word which is often misspelt: there is a single *r*, a double *l* and then a single *l*. Notice that the final *l* does not double in the present participle and past tense: **paralleling**, **paralleled**; this is an exception to the general rule for words ending in *l*.

parliament

Note the *ia* in the second syllable, which is pronounced [*lə*], not *[lyə]* or *[li-ə]*.

part

When the verb **part** means 'to leave, separate', it may be followed by the preposition **from**: *They parted from their friends at the station; The children became parted from their parents in the crowd.* To **part with** means 'to give up, give away', as in *He refused to part with his books when he moved into a smaller house.*

partially see **partly**.

participles

Participles (verb-forms ending in **-ing**, **-ed**, **-en**, etc.) may be used to form adjective phrases relating to nouns which occur in the following main clause of a sentence: *Walking along the road, I happened to see John and his girlfriend; Badly damaged by fire last year, the house is now being rebuilt.* Such participles always relate to the subject of the verb in the main clause. A common error, and one which often passes unnoticed in informal contexts, is to have the participle linked in meaning to some other noun in the sentence: this is often known as a **hanging** or **misrelated participle**. An example of this would be, to rephrase the second sentence above, **Badly damaged by fire last year, I am in the process of rebuilding the house.* It is obvious that what is meant by this sentence is that the house was damaged by fire; however, what the sentence actually says is that 'I' was damaged by fire, since the participle *damaged* must refer to the subject of the following clause, *I*. Similarly, **Crossing the road, a bus knocked me down* is incorrect, since it was clearly 'me', not 'the bus', who was crossing the road. The sentence must be rephrased: either *Crossing the road, I was knocked down by a bus* with the participle referring to the subject of the clause, or *When I was crossing the street, a bus knocked me down* with a full clause replacing the phrase, would be correct and acceptable.

Note that there are a number of words in present-day English which are in origin participles but which are now treated as prepositions and conjunctions, e.g. *considering, speaking (of), talking (of), concerning, barring, excepting, pending, granted, including, following, given, providing, provided, supposing, assuming, seeing.* The above rule linking participles to following subjects does not apply to these words: *Considering the difficulties, you were lucky to finish the job at all; Talking of John, here he comes now; Seeing that you only have three days to complete the job, you had better get started now.*

partly, partially

Partly and **partially** are not synonymous. **Partly** means 'in part or parts, concerning only a part', as in *The house is constructed partly of stone and partly of wood*. **Partially** means 'not to a state of completion', as in *The house is only partially built* (i.e. it is not yet completely built).

past, passed

Passed is the past tense and past participle of the verb **pass**: *He has passed the exam*; *He passed me the salt and pepper*. **Past** is the form to use in all other senses: *There's no use dwelling on the past*; *past participle*; *past mistakes*; *The time for doing that is long past*.

peaceable, peaceful

Do not confuse these two words. **Peaceable** means 'not inclined to fight, not quarrelsome, free from fighting', and is used mostly of people, their temperaments or their behaviour. **Peaceful** means 'calm, without disturbance' and is normally applied to situations, scenes, periods of time, and activities: *a peaceful night's sleep*.

pennies, pence

The plural form **pennies** is used when the emphasis is on coins as separate objects: *a pile of pennies*. **Pence** is used when what is meant is a sum of money: *That will cost six pence*. Since the introduction of decimal coinage in the United Kingdom, **1p** [*wun'-pē'*] or even **1 pence** is sometimes substituted for **penny** in informal contexts: *a pile of 1p's*; *a pile of one-pence pieces*. The form **one pence** should be avoided in formal contexts as it is not considered correct by many people, but it is common and fairly acceptable in informal speech.

people, persons

The normal plural of **person** is **people**. **Persons** is found only in very formal or official contexts, especially in the sense of 'any individual' or 'individuals', as in *Persons wishing to see the mayor must make an appointment with his secretary* and *The police stated that he had been killed by a person or persons unknown*.

perennial see **annual**.

period see **full stop**.

person(s) see **people**.

persona non grata

Persona non grata is a Latin phrase, pronounced [*pər-sōn'ə non grä'tə*], meaning 'a person not liked by or acceptable to (some

99

other person)'. In a formal, technical sense it is applied to a person whose presence in a country is not acceptable to the government of that country (as in *He has been declared persona non grata by the British government*), but it is often used loosely and facetiously, as in *I'm persona non grata with the boss at the moment*. Although singular in form, it may in informal contexts refer back to a plural noun or pronoun (*We're all persona non grata at the moment*), but in formal contexts a plural form **personae non gratae** [*pər-sōn'ē non grä'tē*] should be used.

personnel, personal

Personnel is a noun meaning 'the people employed in a shop, factory, company, etc.' It is a collective noun which should be followed by a plural verb: *Our personnel are very highly trained*. Do not confuse **personnel** (with two *n*'s and an *e*) with the adjective **personal** (one *n* and an *a*).

perturb, disturb

These two verbs both have meanings relating to the causing of disorder or agitation, but they are not completely synonymous or interchangeable in all contexts. **Perturb** means 'to cause anxiety or worry': *His threats did not perturb her in the least*. **Disturb** also has the meaning 'to upset or worry', as in *This news clearly disturbed him greatly*, but has the further meaning 'to irritate, interrupt the work, thoughts or rest of, etc.', as in *His singing doesn't disturb me at all*. If the disruption or agitation is physical rather than mental, **disturb** must be used, not **perturb**: *The violent storm disturbed the surface of the lake*.

phlegm, phlegmatic

Note the *ph* and the *g* in these words. The *g* is silent in **phlegm**, but pronounced in **phlegmatic**.

physician see doctor.

pigmy see pygmy.

piteous, pitiable, pitiful

Pitiful is the commonest of these three adjectives, which are clearly all related to the noun **pity**. It means 'very sad, arousing or deserving pity', as in *She was a pitiful sight*; it also means 'arousing or deserving contempt, very bad, very poor', as in *He made a pitiful attempt at catching the ball*. **Pitiable** is synonymous with **pitiful** but is rather less common: *He was in a pitiable condition; That was a pitiable attempt you made*. **Piteous** is a rather formal or literary word meaning 'arousing or deserving pity', as in *She gave a piteous cry.* **Piteous** must not be used to denote 'arousing or deserving contempt'; only **pitiful** and **pitiable** have this meaning.

plane, 'plane see **aeroplane.**

plurals

The correct formation and spelling of plural nouns is one aspect of English grammar which many people find particularly difficult and confusing, and if one considers such pairs of plurals as *heroes* and *sopranos, passers-by* and *stand-bys, chiefs* and *thieves, moths* and *mouths*, it is not hard to see why so many people make mistakes such as **heros, *thiefs* and **spys* or **spy's*.

The following article is intended to clarify the rules in areas of spelling or plural-formation where there is, or could be, some confusion.

I. Spelling

1. Nouns ending in *o* add either *-es* or *-s* alone in the plural. Nouns ending in *oo*, or in which the final *o* is preceded by another vowel, add *-s: zoos; radios; studios*. Of the other nouns ending in *o*, most add *-s*, but the relatively small group of *-es* words includes most of the commonest of the words which end in *o*. If we take *-s* as the rule, we can then list the *-es* plurals as exceptions. They are as follows: *buffaloes, cargoes, dingoes, dominoes, echoes, embargoes, goes, heroes, mangoes, mottoes, Negroes, noes, potatoes, tomatoes, tornadoes, torpedoes, vetoes,* and *volcanoes.* A number of words may be spelt with either *-s* or *-es: archipelago(e)s, banjo(e)s, grotto(e)s, halo(e)s, innuendo(e)s, memento(e)s, mosquito(e)s,* and *salvo(e)s*.

2. Nouns ending in *y* normally have a plural in *-ies: spy, spies; cry, cries.* Proper names are an exception to this rule: *the two Germanys; the four Marys.* Compound nouns in which the *y* is part of an adverb or preposition are a further exception to the rule: *stand-bys; lay-bys.* If the final *y* is preceded by a vowel, *-s* alone is added to form the plural: *day, days; monkey, monkeys.*

3. Words of French origin which regularly take an *-x* in the plural in French usually do so also in English, although the regular English plural ending *-s* is also possible: *bureau, bureaux* or *bureaus.*

II. Formation of plurals

1. Compound nouns normally pluralize the element which carries the basic noun meaning underlying the compound: *mothers-in-law; passers-by; men-of-war; fountain pens; man-eaters.*

Note however that *mother-in-laws* is common in informal English, that *court martials* is as common as *courts martial*, and that nouns denoting ranks are an exception to the rule (e.g. *sergeant-majors*). When no element of the compound carries the basic noun meaning, the *-s* is added to the last element of the compound: *grown-ups*; *stand-bys*; *gin-and-tonics*.

2. Some nouns ending in *f* alter this to a *v* in the plural: *calf*, *calves*; *knife*, *knives*; and so also *elf*, *half*, *leaf*, *life*, *loaf*, *self*, *sheaf*, *shelf*, *thief*, *wife* and *wolf*. A few nouns may have either *-fs* or *-ves* in the plural: *handkerchief*, *hoof*, *turf*, *wharf*.

3. Words ending in *-is* in the singular normally form their plural by altering *-is* to *-es*: *crisis*, *crises*; *hypothesis*, *hypotheses*. Note however that the plural of *metropolis* is *metropolises*.

4. A number of words of Latin or Greek origin have retained their Latin and Greek plural forms. Some of the commonest of these are listed below (those which are underlined also have regularly-formed plurals in *-s* and *-es*):

antenna, pl. *antennae*, and so also *formula*, *larva*, *nebula*, *pupa*, and *vertebra*; the plural of *alga*, *algae*, is pronounced [al'jē]; *bacillus*, pl. *bacilli*, and so also *cactus*, *fungus* (*fungi* is pronounced [-gī] or [-jī]), *nucleus*, *radius*, *stimulus*, and *stylus*; the normal plural of *syllabus* is *syllabuses*, but *syllabi* does exist also; *genus*, pl. *genera*, and so also *corpus* and *opus*;

aquarium, pl. *aquaria*, and so also *addendum*, *bacterium*, *curriculum*, *memorandum*, *moratorium*, and *symposium*; see also the entries at **medium** and **data**;

phenomenon, pl. *phenomena*, and so also *automaton* and *criterion*; for *appendix* and *index*, see the separate entries for these words.

5. A number of common words have completely irregular plurals: *tooth*, pl. *teeth*; *goose*, *geese*; *foot*, *feet*; *man*, *men*; *woman*, *women*; *mouse*, *mice*; *louse*, *lice*; *child*, *children*; *ox*, *oxen*; *brother*, *brethren* (in the sense of 'religious brothers'); *sheep*, *sheep*; *grouse* (the bird), *grouse*; *salmon*, *salmon*; see also **pence**.

III. Pronunciation

A number of words form plurals in the regular way, but alter their pronunciation in some way not indicated by the spelling of the plural. Note that the *s* of *house* is pronounced [z] in the plural *houses*, and that the [th] is altered to [dh] in *baths*, *mouths*, *paths*, and *youths*, and sometimes also in *oaths*, *sheaths*, *truths*, and *wreaths*.

IV. Animal Names

Most nouns denoting animals and birds form regular plurals: *two monkeys, five cows*, etc. However, a number of nouns denoting animals and birds often hunted for food or sport have both a regular plural and a plural form identical to the singular form. In general the regular plural is used when referring to individual animals, the second type of plural when referring to the animals as a mass or group: *two antelopes, a herd of antelope; three ducks, a flock of wild duck; two fish* or *two fishes, a shoal of fish.*

For other notes on plurals, see -**ful**, -**ics**, and **abbreviations**.

politic, political

Political means 'pertaining to politics': *the political system of the country; political parties.* **Politic** is a rather formal word meaning 'wise, sensible', as in *a politic decision; He considered it politic to leave before further trouble developed.*

The adverb formed from **political** is **politically**; the adverb corresponding to **politic** is **politicly**.

practicable, practical

Like their opposites **impracticable** and **impractical**, these two words are often confused. **Practicable** means 'able to be done, used, or carried out': *a practicable plan.* **Practical**, when applied to things, suggestions, etc. also means 'able to be done, used, or carried out' but has the further connotation of 'efficient, sensible': *Both these suggested courses of action are practicable, but John's is certainly the more practical of the two.* Applied to people, **practical** means 'able to do, make, or deal with things well or efficiently'.

practice, practise see -ce, -se.

pray see prey.

precede see proceed.

precipitate, precipitous

Precipitous is a very formal word meaning 'very steep, like a precipice': *The path through the mountains is narrow and precipitous.* **Precipitate**, also a rather formal word, means 'hasty', often 'too hasty': *a precipitate decision.*

prefer, preferable

Prefer should be followed by **to**, not *than: *I prefer tea to coffee*, not *I prefer tea than coffee.* The same rule applies to **preferable**: *Tea is preferable to coffee.*

The stress on **preferable** should be on the first syllable.

prescribe, proscribe

Confusion between these two verbs may lead one to say the exact opposite of what one intends. To **prescribe** is to advise or order, to **proscribe** is to ban, outlaw, or forbid: *the books prescribed for study on this course*; *This book was formerly proscribed by the Church*; *The law prescribes certain penalties for this offence*; *Such actions are proscribed by law*.

presume see assume.

prevent

The correct constructions with the verb **prevent** are **prevent from** plus a verb in **-ing** or **prevent** plus a possessive adjective or noun and a verb ending in **-ing**: *The storm prevented me from leaving*; *The storm prevented my leaving*. Construction with a noun or pronoun followed by a verb in **-ing** (*The storm prevented me leaving*) is acceptable in informal contexts but should be avoided in formal speech and writing.

prey, pray

Prey is that which a bird or animal hunts and kills for food: *The lion carried off its prey*. **Prey** can also be used as a verb: *Hawks prey on smaller birds*; *Fears preyed on her mind*. To **pray** is to say a prayer: *She prayed to God to help her*.

principal, principle

These two words are one of the most frequently confused and misspelt pair of words in English. As an adjective, **principal** means 'most important': *Shipbuilding is one of Britain's principal industries*. As a noun **principal** means 'the head of a school, college or university' or 'the leading actor, singer or dancer in a theatrical production'. The word **principle** can only be used as a noun. It means 'a general rule' or 'the theory underlying a method or way of working': *the principles of economic theory*; *the principle of the jet engine*; *I agree with the idea in principle*; *He refused to do it on principle*; *It is against my principles to borrow money*.

privilege

Note the spelling of this frequently misspelt word.

proceed, precede

Proceed and **precede** are often confused, and where not confused, misspelt. Note the spelling of the second syllable of each of these words. (For further comments on **-ceed** and **-cede**, see the entry at **-cede**.)

To **proceed** is 'to continue, to go on, to begin to do something or follow a course of action': *They proceeded with their work*; *They proceeded to ask a lot of stupid questions*. To **precede** is 'to go before': *She preceded him into the room*; *He is mentioned in this chapter and also in the preceding one*.

professor

Note the single *f* and double *s*.

In British English, a **professor** is the head of a university department. In American English, a **professor** is any university lecturer.

programme, program

Programme is the usual British spelling of this word, **program** the American. However, the spelling **program** is used in British English in the context of computer technology.

Note that in American English, the present participle and past tense and participle of **program** are **programing**, **programed** or **programming**, **programmed**, but that in computer technology the *m* is always doubled.

prone see **liable**.

pronunciation

Note that this word is not***pronounciation**.

prophecy, prophesy see -ce, -se, etc.

proscribe see **prescribe**.

publicly

Politic and **public** are the only adjectives ending in -*ic* which add -*ly* rather than -*ally* to form adverbs. ***Publically** is a common error; **publicly** is the correct form.

purposely, purposefully

Purposely means 'on purpose, intentionally'. **Purposefully** means 'with, or as if with, a definite purpose in mind; in a determined manner', as in *He strode purposefully along the corridor*.

pygmy, pigmy

Both forms of this word are correct, but the spelling with *y* rather than *i* is preferred by most people.

quiz

Note that this word doubles the *z* in the plural of the noun and the past tense and present and past participles of the verb: *quizzes*, *quizzed*, *quizzing*.

quotation marks

There is little that needs to be said with regard to quotation marks (also known as 'inverted commas'). They are used to mark off quoted speech and to separate off or highlight words or phrases in sentences:

'Do come in,' he said.

What does 'an accessary after the fact' mean?

Both single and double quotes are correct, but modern usage prefers single quotes. However, if there is a quotation or highlighted passage within another quotation, both single and double quotes must be used:

'What does "an accessary after the fact" mean?' he asked.

Punctuation marks that belong to or are part of the quoted material should be kept within the quotation marks, while other punctuation marks are placed outside the quotes. A full stop is replaced by a comma when it stands at the end of a quote which is not the end of the whole sentence. The following examples show these rules in operation:

He said: 'You must help her.'

'You must help her,' he said.

'You', he said, 'must help her.'

'You, John, must help her,' he said.

'You, John,' he said, 'must help her.'

'Must I help her?' he asked.

'What do you mean by "an accessary after the fact"?' he asked.

If the end of a quotation is also the end of the sentence of which the quotation is part, there should be no full stop at the end of the sentence if there is already a full stop or other punctuation mark at the end of the quotation:

He said: 'You must help her.' is correct;

He said: 'You must help her.'. is wrong.

With question marks and exclamation marks, the rule is not absolute: for example, a sentence like

'Did he say "Are you coming?"?' she asked.

is possible, but it is generally considered preferable to omit one or other of the question marks, even though this is not strictly logical since there are two separate questions in the sentence.

receipt

Note the *ei* and the *p* in this word.

refute, deny

To **deny** means 'to declare (something) not to be true': *He denied* *that he had stolen the money.* Strictly speaking, **refute** means 'to prove or show (something) to be untrue': *You can easily refute his arguments.* Unfortunately, **refute** is now used by many people to mean 'to deny strongly'. This has rendered the word almost useless, as one is often not quite certain, when it is said, for example, that allegations have been refuted, whether the allegations have been proved wrong or merely emphatically denied. To avoid ambiguity, expecially in written material, it is necessary either to avoid the word **refute** altogether, or to make sure that there is sufficient information in the rest of the passage to make the intended meaning clear.

regal, royal

Regal means 'like or suitable for a king or queen': *regal splendour*; *regal bearing*. **Royal** means 'of a king or queen': *the Royal Family*; *a royal decree*. Occasionally, **royal** is used in the sense of **regal** given above, e.g. 'splendid', 'magnificent': *a royal feast*.

regard

Both **with regard to** and **in regard to**, meaning 'about, concerning', are correct, but the former is commoner than the latter. **As regards** (with the verb **regard**) is also correct. All three phrases are rather formal, and it is often better to use a simple preposition like **about** instead. Note that **in** and **with** are not always interchangeable with **regard**: **in this regard** is correct, **with this regard** is not.

Regard to must not be confused with **regard for**. Followed by **to**, **regard** means 'reference', as in *with regard to*, or 'attention'; as in the rather formal expression *have/pay regard* to (= to take into account, consider, pay attention to). Followed by **for**, **regard** means 'concern, care, respect', as in *Have you no regard for my feelings?*; *I have great regard for him.*

regretful, regrettable

Regretful means 'full of regret, sad, sorry'; **regrettable** means 'causing regret, to be regretted': *It is regrettable that you have behaved so foolishly, and I feel most regretful that I must now ask you to go.*

relation

Both **in relation to** and **with relation to** are correct. Like the corresponding phrases with **regard**, these phrases are formal and are often better replaced by simple prepositions like **about**.

relation, relative

In the sense of 'a person to whom one is related', these two words

107

remittance, remission

are synonymous and interchangeable. Some authorities do suggest certain differences in meaning or connotation between these words, but since no two of them agree on what the differences are, one may justifiably conclude that such distinctions as they do discern are matters of personal whim or preference rather than established English usage.

remittance, remission

These two nouns correspond to different senses of the verb **remit**, and should not be confused. **Remittance** is a formal word for the sending of money in payment for something, or the money itself: *We are grateful for your remittance·of the correct sum of money*; *Thank you for your remittance*. **Remission** means 'a lessening in force or effect' (as in *Remissions in that form of cancer are not unknown*), 'the shortening of a prison sentence', 'the cancelling of a debt or punishment', and, in Christian theology, 'the forgiveness (of sins)'.

repetitive, repetitious

These two adjectives are both obviously related to the noun **repetition**. They are very similar in meaning but differ slightly in use. **Repetitious** is normally applied to speech or writing and always carries the connotation of excessive or tedious repetition: *I'm tired of listening to his repetitious lectures*. **Repetitive** may be applied to speech and writing or to actions, activities, etc. It may, like **repetitious**, have a connotation of tedium, but it may also be used in a more neutral sense, meaning simply 'characterized by repetition': *This work is of a very repetitive nature*; *I realize that what I am saying is rather repetitive, but I do want to make sure that you grasp the point*.

replace see **substitute.**

request

The verb **request** means 'to ask for'. It is therefore incorrect to say or write **request for**. The correct construction is to **request** something **from** someone: *Many people have requested this next song*; *The Tax Office has requested information about your salary from the company secretary.*

respect

The correct prepositional constructions are **with respect to** and **in respect of**. On the preferability of simple prepositions like **about**, see the comments at **regard** and **relation**.

respective

The adverb **respectively** is used to show the correct one-to-one relationship between people or things in two groups or lists mentioned one after the other. For example, in *John, Mary and Peter bought a book, a record and a pen respectively*, the word **respectively** serves to indicate that John bought a book, Mary bought a record and Peter bought a pen.

Similarly, the adjective respective means 'each to, for, with, etc. his own': *Peter and George went to their respective homes* (= Peter went to Peter's home and George went to George's).

responsible

Note that in most contexts the opposite of **responsible** is **not responsible**, not **irresponsible**. *He was not responsible for his actions* and *I will not be responsible for that dog* are correct. *'He was irresponsible for his actions* and *'I will be irresponsible for that dog* are not.

restrain see constrain.

revenge see avenge.

review, revue

A **revue** is a type of amusing theatre show. A **review** is a report, study or critical consideration of something: *Have you seen the review of his latest novel in today's paper?*; *We'll have a review of her progress at the end of the month.*

reward see award.

rhyme, rhythm

Do not forget the *h* after the *r* in these words.

round see around.

royal see regal.

's see of.

say

Note that **says** and **said** are pronounced [*sez*] and [*sed*] respectively, not *[*sāz*] and *[*sād*].

sceptic

Sceptic is pronounced [*skep'tik*]. In American English, the word is written with a *k*, **skeptic**. For the difference between a **cynic** and a **sceptic**, see **cynic**.

schedule

This word is pronounced [*shed'ūl*] in British English, [*sked'ūl*] in American English.

Scottish, Scotch, Scots

Scottish is the normal adjective meaning 'of or belonging to Scotland': *He is Scottish, not English*; *an exhibition of Scottish books*. **Scotch** should only be applied to certain products, or supposed products, of Scotland: *Scotch eggs*; *Scotch pine*; *Scotch terrier*; *Scotch thistle*. The adjective **Scots** is also more restricted in use than **Scottish**: it is used in *Scots law* (which is different from English law), *Scots pine* (= *Scotch pine*), the *Scots language*, and in the names of certain army regiments.

scream, screech, shriek

Note the spelling of these words, all three pronounced with an [ē] but correctly spelt *ea*, *ee* and *ie* respectively.

There are slight differences in meaning between **scream**, **screech** and **shriek**. The normal word for a loud, rather high-pitched cry is **scream**: *She screamed with pain*; *She gave a scream of pain*. **Shriek** usually denotes a cry that is shorter, sharper, and more high-pitched than a scream, and often implies more intense pain or fear than that which gives rise to a scream. A **screech** is similar to a **shriek**, but harsher and more strident: *The parrots were screeching in their cages*. All these words may be applied to the sounds made by machinery and other objects: *He drove round the corner with tyres screaming*; *the screech of brakes*; *the shriek of a factory siren*.

-se *in nouns and verbs* see **-ce.**

-sede see -cede.

seek

Seek is a rather formal or literary word meaning 'to look for'. It is incorrect to say **seek for*.

semicolon

A **semicolon** is used to mark a pause or break in a sentence greater than that indicated by a comma but less than the complete break marked by a full stop. It is generally used to separate parts of a sentence which are of more or less equal importance but which are not linked by a conjunction (such as *and*, *or*, *but*, etc.): *To err is human; to forgive, divine*.

There are two instances in which a semicolon may correctly be substituted for a comma:

1. If a sentence consists of a number of long clauses, themselves including several commas, the clauses may be separated by semicolons rather than commas in the interests of clarity.

2. Semicolons may used to subdivide into groups items in a list some of which are separated by commas, since the use of commas alone might not show clearly the intended subgroupings: *Among the area's chief industries are shipbuilding, automobile engineering, and steel manufacturing; textiles and clothing; coalmining; and brewing.*

sensual, sensuous

These two adjectives, which both refer to what is experienced through the senses, are frequently confused. **Sensuous** means 'perceived by or affecting the senses, especially in a pleasant way', as in *I find his music very sensuous; Her sculptures have a certain sensuous quality.* **Sensual** means 'of or concerning the senses and the body rather than the mind', and is often used in a derogatory sense suggesting an excessive fondness for bodily pleasures, especially sexual pleasure.

separate

This word is often misspelt **seperate*. Note the correct spelling.

septic

Do not confuse this word with **sceptic**. **Septic** means 'full of, or caused by, germs that are poisoning the blood': *a septic finger/wound; septic poisoning.* For **sceptic**, see **cynic**.

shade, shadow

Shade and **shadow** are in origin forms of the same word. In present-day English, **shade** refers to an area of relative darkness affording shelter from light and heat (especially of the sun) caused by the blocking of light by some object or objects: *The trees provided some shade from the sun; I prefer to sit in the shade.* **Shadow** is usually used for a particular patch of comparative darkness created by some object blocking off the light (from whatever source), especially when the darker patch is relatively small and clearly mirrors in outline the object causing it: *We are in the shadow of that building; He could see her shadow on the curtains.* Notice that **shade** very often has connotations of shelter or protection which **shadow** does not have.

shall, will

In its simplest form, the rule governing the use of **shall** and **will** is as follows: to express a simple future tense, use **shall** with *I* or *we*, **will** with *you, he, they*, etc.; to express permission, obligation, determination, compulsion, etc., use **will** with *I* and *we*, **shall** elsewhere. The following examples demonstrate this rule: *I shall* *be glad when this book is finished; Shall we see you again next week?; They will be very angry; I will not do it!; You shall go whether you want to or not; You shall have a bicycle if you pass your exams; I am determined that they shall never do that again.*

There are, however, many exceptions to this basic rule:

1. **Will** is often used with *I* and *we* to indicate a simple future tense: *I will be glad when this book is finished.* This use of **will** is very widespread and generally acceptable, but is best still avoided in formal written English. Note that in questions with *I*, **shall** is generally used, not **will**; *Shall I come in now?* The tendency to use **will** rather than **shall** is greater among speakers of American English and Scottish and Irish speakers of British English, whereas **shall** is preferred by many of the speakers of British English living in England.

2. **Shall** is often used with *I* and *we* to express the speaker's firm intentions, or to ask for instructions: *We shall overcome; We shall fight them on the beaches; What shall we drink?; Shall I tell him or shan't I?*

shame

In the sense of 'an unpleasant feeling caused by awareness of one's own or someone else's guilt, fault, foolishness or failure', **shame** may be followed by **at** or **for**: *I feel no shame for what I have done; He felt no shame at having behaved in the way he had; I was full of shame at his rudeness.* In the sense of 'a cause for regret or matter for blame', **shame** is followed by **to** and an infinitive: *It's a shame to treat a dog like that.*

should, would

The rules governing the use of **should** and **would** are a little more complicated than those for **shall** and **will**, but are nonetheless fairly straightforward:

1. As past tense equivalents of **shall** and **will**, **should** is generally used where **shall** would be used for a simple future and **would** where **will** would be used: *I said I should see him tomorrow; He said he would see him tomorrow.* Those who would say *I/we will* for a future tense would say *I/we would* rather than *I/we should: I said I would see him tomorrow.* **Would** is sometimes preferred to **should** even by those who would use **shall** rather than **will**, in order to avoid ambiguities arising from the other senses of **should** listed below.

2. The same distribution of **should** and **would** is found in main clauses linked to conditional clauses (e.g. clauses begin-

ning with **if**): *If we had not caught the bus, we should not have got there on time; If he had missed the bus, he would have been late.* In such cases also, **would** is often preferred to **should**: *If we had not caught the bus, we would not have got there on time.*

3. **Would** rather than **should** is used with **rather** and **sooner**: *I would rather stay here.*

4. **Should** is correctly used in the 1st, 2nd and 3rd persons in the sense of 'ought to': *I know I should go but I don't want to; He really should stop smoking; They should be there by now.* **Should** is also used to express doubtful or tentative conditions (as in *Let me know if he should happen to arrive*) and after expressions of surprise, sorrow or other emotions (as in *I am very sorry that this should have happened; It is quite unthinkable that he should get off scot-free*).

5. **Would** is used in the 1st, 2nd, and 3rd persons when it denotes habitual actions or determination: *We would always have bacon and eggs for breakfast in those days; He would often go for a long walk after supper; You would insist on going out without a coat and hat; It's my own fault — I would insist on going there alone.* **Would** is also used with constructions such as **if only**, expressing desires or the agreement or other conditions necessary for something desirable: *If only he would come; If we would only stop arguing for a moment, we might realize that there is really nothing worth arguing about* (compare *If we should ever stop arguing, we should/would have nothing to say to each other*).

A common mistake found with **should** and **would** when referring to the past is the creation of a 'double past tense' construction when a single past tense is all that is required. For example, **I should have liked to have been there* has two past tenses, *should have liked* and *have been*. The correct construction would only have one, either *I should like to have been there* or *I should have liked to be there*.

shriek see **scream**.

shrunk, shrunken

Shrunk is the past participle of the verb **shrink**: *My shirts have shrunk in the wash.* **Shrunken** is used as an adjective: *The cannibals had decorated their huts with shrunken heads; He had suddenly become old and shrunken.*

since see **ago**.

skilful

Note the single *l* of *skil-* and *-ful*. In American English, this word is correctly spelt **skillful**.

slander see **libel.**

small see **little.**

smile

The normal preposition used after the verb **smile** is **at**: *She smiled at me as she went past*. **Smile on** is a rather literary expression meaning 'to favour', and is usually applied to luck, fate, fortune, etc. thought of as people: *Fate smiled on us and we reached land safely*.

so ... as see **as ... as.**

sociable, social

The adjective **sociable** is usually applied to people and means 'friendly, fond of the company of others': *Our new neighbours aren't very sociable*; *He's a cheerful, sociable person*. **Social** means 'of or concerning society', as in *Problems such as this are social rather than medical* and *social class*, or 'concerning the gathering together or meeting of people for recreation and amusement' as in *a social club* and *His reasons for calling round were purely social*.

sort of see **kind of.**

so therefore

The expression **so therefore** is heard more and more frequently nowadays, where **so** or **therefore** alone would be quite sufficient: **There was no-one in the office, so therefore I just left a note on the desk and went out again*. Although examples of **so therefore** often pass unnoticed in informal speech, it is better to avoid such an unnecessary and tautological construction. It must certainly never be used in formal speech and writing.

speak

The verb **speak** is most often followed by the prepositions **to** and **about**, as in *I was speaking to John about that only yesterday*. To **speak with** may be used instead of **speak to**, but this is more common in American English than British English.

To **speak of** is 'to mention, refer to', as in *He never speaks of his late wife*. To **speak on** is 'to give a lecture on', as in *He will be speaking on the fungi of Europe this evening*.

In formal contexts, **speak to** may mean 'to speak about or in support of', as in *The Chairman called on him to speak to his proposal*.

speak, speech

Note the difference in the spelling of these words: *ea* for **speak** but *ee* for **speech**.

specially see **especially.**

specialty, speciality
To all intents and purposes, these two words are synonymous. **Speciality** is the commoner form in British English, **specialty** in American English.

speech see **speak.**

spelling rules
Many spelling problems have been dealt with in individual entries in this book. This article on spelling is intended only to cover certain important points of spelling not covered elsewhere.

I Verbs

1. The present participle of a verb is formed by adding -*ing* to it: *walk, walking; sing, singing; stay, staying.* If the verb ends in a single consonant which is preceded by a single vowel written with a single letter and the stress of the word is on the final syllable, the final consonant is doubled: *run, running; swim, swimming; prefer, preferring;* but *enter, entering* (the *r* is not doubled as the stress is not on the final syllable of *enter*); *scream, screaming* (*m* is not doubled as the vowel preceding it is written with a double letter); *initial, initialing* (*l* does not double because it is preceded by two vowels).

There are unfortunately a few exceptions to this rule. The final consonant of a compound word is doubled if it would be doubled when not part of a compound: *whip, whipping* so *horsewhip, horsewhipping.* A final *l* preceded by a single-letter vowel doubles in British spelling irrespective of the position of the stress, but in American English *l* follows the general rule given above and doubles only if the final syllable is stressed: *signal,* Brit. *signalling,* Amer. *signaling; tunnel,* Brit. *tunnelling,* Amer. *tunneling,* but note that *paralleling* is correct in both British and American English. Most verbs ending in *p* follow the general rule, but in British English a few double the final *p*: *worship, worshipping; kidnap, kidnapping; handicap, handicapping.* Certain other words double the final letter contrary to what would be expected from the general rule: *humbug, humbugging; leapfrog, leapfrogging; zigzag, zigzagging; hobnob, hobnobbing;* and *program* (in the computer science sense), *programming.* A few words allow both single and doubled consonants before -*ing*: *bias, biasing* or *biassing; bus, busing* or *bussing; focus, focusing* or *focussing; leaflet, leafleting* or *leafletting.*

Verbs ending in *c* generally add *k* before -*ing*: *picnic, picnicking.*

Two exceptions to this are *arc*, *arcing* and *talc*, *talcing*.

Verbs ending in a silent *e* drop the *e* before adding *-ing*: *bake*, *baking*; *refine*, *refining*; *queue*, *queuing*. Verbs ending in *ee*, *oe* and *ye* are exceptions to this rule, and do not drop the final *e*: *agree*, *agreeing*; *hoe*, *hoeing*; *dye*, *dyeing*. A few words retain the final *e* in order to be distinguishable from similar words with no *e*: compare *singe*, *singeing* and *sing*, *singing*, and similarly *routeing*, *swingeing*, and *tingeing*. The verb *age* allows both *ageing* and *aging*.

2. The rules for the formation of past tenses and past participles in *-ed* are essentially the same as for the formation of present participles in *-ing*: if a consonant is doubled or remains single in the formation of the present participle, the same will apply in the past tense and past participle: *prefer*, *preferring*, *preferred*; *scream*, *screaming*, *screamed*; *worship*, *worshipping*, *worshipped*; *zigzag*, *zigzagging*, *zigzagged*. Similarly, verbs ending in *c* add *k*: *picnic*, *picnicked*.

Verbs ending in *e* drop the *e* in all cases before *-ed*: *bake*, *baked*; *queue*, *queued*; *agree*, *agreed*, not *agreeed*; *hoe*, *hoed*; *dye*, *dyed*, *die*, *died*. Verbs ending in *y* preceded by a consonant change the *y* to *i* but do not do so if the *y* is preceded by a vowel: *cry*, *cried*; but *stay*, *stayed*; *prey*, *preyed*. (Note that *said*, *paid* and *laid* are exceptions to this last rule.)

3. There is little that needs to be said with regard to third person verb-forms of the present tense. Verbs ending in *y* which change *y* to *i* in the past tense do so also in the present tense: *cry*, *cries*; *marry*, *marries*, but *stay*, *stays*.

4. See also **-ise, -ize**; **-ce, -se**.

II Nouns

1. Nouns ending in *-er* formed from verbs follow the same rules as participles with regard to doubling of consonants, dropping the final *e*'s, the changing of *y* to *i*, etc.: *run*, *runner*; *write*, *writer*; *dream*, *dreamer*; *cry*, *crier*; *picnic*, *picnicker*. Note, however, that both *flier* and *flyer*, and *drier* and *dryer*, are correct. See also **-er, -or, -ar**.

2. Noun suffixes which begin with a consonant (e.g. *-ment*, *-ness*) generally do not cause any alteration to the root-word to which they are added: *arrange*, *arrangement*; *white*, *whiteness*; *false*, *falsehood*. Note however that the final *e* of *argue* is dropped in *argument*, and that the final *e* of *judge*, *abridge* and *acknowledge* may be dropped in *judgement/judgment*, etc.

The final *y* of adjectives like *silly* changes to *i* before *-ness*, e.g. *silly*, *silliness*; *sultry*, *sultriness*; if the *y* is pronounced [ī], it does not change to *i*: *dry*, *dryness*; *sly*, *slyness*. Note that the noun formed from *busy* is often written *busyness*, in order to distinguish it from *business* which has developed its own meanings. Nouns in *-ness* formed from adjectives ending in *-ey* pose particular problems: some retain the *-ey*, some alter the *-ey* to *-i-*, and some allow both forms, and authorities differ on which adjectives belong to which group. However, since most of the common words of this group often or always alter *-ey* to *-i-*, it is recommended that the reader take this as the general rule: *clayey, clayiness*; *matey, matiness*; *phoney, phoniness*.

3. See also **plurals**.

III Adjectives

1. Adjectives ending in *-ish* and *-y* follow much the same rules as participles of verbs with regard to doubling of consonants, dropping of *e*, etc.: *dream, dreamy*; *gossip, gossipy*; *grit, gritty*; *pal, pally*; *bone, bony*; *green, greenish*; *red, reddish*; *blue, bluish*; *dry, dryish*; *gray, grayish*. Note, however, that in words ending in *-ue*, the *e* does not drop before *-y*, e.g. *glue, gluey*, and that the *e* is retained in a number of other cases also e.g. *cagey, dicey, matey, pricey*. Notice especially the difference between *holey* (= full of holes) and *holy* (= sacred).

2. Adjective suffixes such as *-ful* which begin with a consonant do not usually cause any alterations in the root-word to which they are added: *use, useful*; *care, careless*; *spot, spotless*. Note, however, the loss of the *e* of *awe* in *awful*.

3. See also **-able, -ible**; **comparison of adjectives and adverbs**.

IV Adverbs

Adverbs are generally formed by adding *-ly* to an adjective: *foolish, foolishly*; *surprising, surprisingly*; *initial, initially*; *strange, strangely*; *free, freely*. Certain categories of words are, however, exceptions to this rule.

1. Adjectives ending in *-ic* add *-ally* to form adverbs: *basic, basically*; *economic, economically* (but see **politic** and **public**).

2. Adjectives ending in *-le* preceded by one or more consonants generally drop the *e* and add *y*: *simple, simply*; *subtle, subtly*; *single, singly*; *double, doubly*; *supple, supply*.

3. *True, due* and *whole* drop their final *e* before adding *-ly*: *truly*; *duly*; *wholly*. *Gay* has the adverb *gaily*.

4. Adjectives ending in *y* alter this *y* to *-i* before *-ly*: *silly*, *sillily*; *weary*, *wearily*. Certain adjectives ending in *y* which is pronounced [ī] may have either *y* or *i* before *-ly*: *dry*, *drily* or *dryly*; *shy*, *shily* or *shyly*; *sly*, *slily* or *slyly*; but only *spryly* and *wryly* are correct, not **sprily* or **wrily*.

A number of adjectives which end in *-ly* are clearly formed by the addition of this *-ly* (an adjective suffix) to another word: *friend*, *friendly*; *heaven*, *heavenly*; *scholar*, *scholarly*. These adjectives do not normally form adverbs in *-ly*, as forms such as *friendlily*, although grammatically correct, sound awkward and are generally avoided by the use of longer expressions such as *in a friendly way*.

5. See also **-ed in adjectives and adverbs**.

V Miscellaneous rules

1. A well-known and very useful rule is the one which runs '*i* before *e* except after *c*'. This applies only to words which are pronounced [*e*]: *believe*, *chief*, *siege*, but *ceiling*, *deceive*, *receipt*. Among the exceptions which have *ei* where *ie* would be expected are: *caffeine*, *codeine*, *counterfeit*, *either*, *inveigle*, *neither*, *protein*, *seize*, *weir*, *weird*, and the name of the island of *Madeira*. One word which has *ie* where *ei* would be expected is *species*.

2. Nouns ending in *-our* drop the *u* before the suffix *-ant*, *-ation*, *-iferous*, *-fic*, *-ise/-ize* and *-ous*, but not before *-able*, *-er*, *-ism*, *-ist*, *-ite* and other suffixes: e.g. *glamour*, *glamorous*, *glamorize*; *humour*, *humorous*; *odour*, *deodorize*, *deodorant*; but *honour*, *honourable*; *favour*, *favourite*.

See also the article on **American spelling** and the various entries throughout the dictionary which deal with particular problems.

split infinitive

An infinitive is the part of a verb which occurs with **to**: *to walk*; *to run*; *to sing*. A split infinitive is a construction in which an adverb stands between **to** and the following verb, as in *Are you willing to really try to do it*? Although split infinitives are condemned or deprecated by many people, there is in fact no reason at all to avoid them. They are not incorrect grammatically, nor are they undesirable from a stylistic point of view. If the most natural, most logical, and most unambiguous position for an adverb in a sentence is between **to** and a verb, that is where the adverb should be put.

start see **begin.**

stationary, stationery

> **Stationary** is an adjective, meaning 'not moving': *a stationary vehicle.* **Stationery** is a noun meaning 'paper, envelopes, etc.': *This firm spends far too much money on stationery.*

stimulant, stimulus

> Both these nouns are related to the verb **stimulate**, and both refer to something which promotes or produces an increase in activity. **Stimulant** is normally used only of a drug or medicine which makes a person more alert or part of his body more active: *Tea and coffee contain stimulants; a powerful heart stimulant.* **Stimulant** may also be used figuratively: *A visit to the art gallery is the best stimulant I know.* A **stimulus** is something which causes a reaction in a living thing: *Light is the stimulus that causes a flower to open.* **Stimulus** is often used to mean 'something which causes or encourages a person to make greater efforts': *Many people think that children need the stimulus of competition to make them work well at school.*

straight, strait

> These words are sometimes confused. **Straight** is generally used as an adjective: *a straight line; Your tie isn't straight; It was so funny I could hardly keep my face straight when I was telling him; I can never get a straight answer from him.* **Straight** may also be used as an adverb meaning 'in a straight line, not bending, curving or wandering' and as a noun meaning 'the straight part of something': *Go straight home; He walked straight across the garden; The horses are in the final straight* (= the straight part of a racecourse). **Straight** is also used in compounds and phrases such as *straightforward, straight away,* and *the straight and narrow.*
> **Strait** is an old adjective meaning 'narrow', 'confined' or 'confining'. It is now found only in compound words such as *strait-jacket* and *strait-laced.* As a noun, **strait** is still in common use, especially in the plural. It means 'a narrow strip of sea between two pieces of land' as in *the Straits of Gibraltar* and *the Bering Strait,* or 'difficulty, need' as in *She had been in great straits financially since her husband died* and *in dire straits.*

style

> It is quite impossible to give clear rules on style. The style one adopts in speaking and writing will, and should, vary to suit one's situation, one's purpose, and one's audience. In writing or speaking in a formal context, one must be careful to avoid slang

and colloquialisms; in writing for or speaking to a general audience, one must take care to avoid using technical jargon understood only by experts in a particular field.

All that will be given here is a few comments worth noting when one is writing or speaking formally, e.g. in reports, business letters, speeches, and so on.

1. Do not use contracted verb-forms such as *he'll, can't, I'd,* etc. Always use the full forms *he will, cannot,* etc.

2. While one must avoid slang and colloquialisms, it is not necessary to search for formal words to replace every 'ordinary' word. Most everyday words are as appropriate in formal contexts as in informal ones. There is no shame in using words like *buy, go* and *stop* and no necessity to replace them with *purchase, proceed,* or *cease.* There is no need to use a phrase such as *with regard to* or *in connection with* when a single word like *about* would serve your purpose just as well.

3. Make sure that your sentences are not so long or so complicated that they obscure the meaning of what is being said. A complex, convoluted sentence may look impressive, but as a general rule, what is not easy to understand has not been well said and should be rephrased in a simpler and more intelligible way.

4. Avoid clichés and stereotyped phrases unless you are sure that they are the best possible way of saying what you want to say. For some people, the use of clichés is a substitute for careful thought, and for this reason clichés are frequently condemned by those who write on good and bad style. But the line between an unacceptable cliché and an acceptable idiomatic expression is not easy to draw, and what one person condemns as a cliché may perhaps be regarded by another person as an idiom which exactly conveys the particular meaning or connotations he wishes to convey in a particular context.

subjunctive

Apart from its obligatory use in certain set expressions such as *as it were, be that as it may, long live the Queen, so be it,* and *suffice it to say,* the subjunctive mood of verbs is not very common in present-day English. In most cases, the subjunctive form of a verb is identical to the indicative form (the form used in ordinary statements), and therefore most people are aware of subjunctives only in the cases where subjunctive forms (as in *if I were you, if he were here, if that be the case*) differ from the corresponding indicative forms (as *I was, he was, that is the case*), and sometimes not even then.

There are two main uses of the subjunctive in English, both more or less restricted to formal language and replaced by other constructions in less formal contexts:

1. After verbs and other constructions denoting commands or requests: *It is imperative that he resign now* (not *resigns*, therefore subjunctive); *I insist that he do it at once* (not *does*). In cases where the subjunctive and indicative forms are identical (e.g. in the third person plural), this construction can lead to ambiguities: in *He suggests that children learn how language works by studying grammar*, it is not clear whether *learn* is an indicative, in which case he is suggesting that this is how children do learn language, or a subjunctive, in which case he is suggesting that this is how they should learn language. If the second meaning is intended, *learn* would be better replaced by *should learn*, which is unambiguous. In non-formal contexts, *should* or an indicative verb is commonly substituted for a subjunctive.

2. A subjunctive verb may be used after **if** and certain other conjunctions in expressions involving hypotheses, suggestions and concessions: *Even if he were here, we wouldn't recognize him*; *Whatever be the reason for his disappearance, I'm sure he hasn't been murdered*. In less formal language, an indicative verb is often used instead of a subjunctive: *Even if he was here, we wouldn't recognize him*.

Note that when what follows **if** refers to a possible event rather than a purely hypothetical one, the verb should be in the indicative: *If he was here yesterday, there is no sign of it now*. (In general, if the following clause contains *would* or *should*, the verb of the **if** clause will, or may, be in the subjunctive; otherwise, it will be in the indicative.)

subsequent see **consequent**.

substitute, replace

If X is put in the place of Y, X is **substituted for** or **replaces** Y and Y is **replaced by** or **with** X. A sentence like *We had to substitute Y by X* is incorrect.

sunk, sunken

The past participle of the verb **sink** is **sunk**: *Six ships have been sunk.* **Sunken** is used only as an adjective: *a sunken ship; sunken cheeks.*

superior

When **superior** means 'better' or 'more important', it behaves like a comparative adjective, but unlike true comparative adjectives, it must never be followed by ***than**, always by **to**: *Is a captain superior to a commander in the Navy?*; *This carpet is far superior to that one* (compare *This carpet is much better than that one*).

In the sense of 'disdainful, showing that one considers oneself better than others', **superior** behaves as an ordinary adjective and may form a comparative and superlative in the normal way: *She had a most superior smile on her face*; *I can put on a more superior air than her if I want to.*

superlative see **comparison of adjectives and adverbs.**

supplement see **complement.**

surgeon see **doctor.**

surprised

Surprised may be followed by **by**, **at** or **to**. **Surprised by** implies a sudden shock caused by something quite unexpected: *When she went into the house, she was surprised by a burglar.* **Surprised at** (followed by a verb ending in **-ing**) and **surprised to** (followed by an infinitive) both imply that the surprise involves less of a shock than that referred to by **surprised by**: *I was surprised at seeing him at the party*; *I was surprised to see him there.* **Surprised at** followed by a noun or pronoun implies an element of censure or reproof: *I'm surprised at you, hitting a little girl like that.*

swap, swop

Both spellings are correct, but **swop** is now commoner than **swap**.

swat, swot

Unlike **swap** and **swop**, **swat** and **swot** are not variant spellings of the same word. They are two quite separate words which must not be confused. **Swat** means 'to hit' and is applied especially to the hitting of flies, wasps and other insects: *He swatted the fly with a folded newspaper.* **Swot** is a colloquial term for 'to study': *She stayed in her room and swotted for her exam.*

sympathize, sympathy, sympathetic

The verb **sympathize** is always followed by the preposition **with**: *I find it hard to sympathize with him when so many of his problems are due to his own stupidity.*

Sympathy may be followed by **for** or **with**. In the sense of 'pity', it is usually followed by **for**: *It is Mary I feel sympathy for, not her husband.* In the sense of 'the state of being in agreement with, or of being able to understand, the attitudes or feelings of another person', **sympathy** is followed by **with**: *The other unions are in sympathy with the railwaymen and back their claim for higher wages.*

Sympathetic means 'feeling or showing sympathy' in both senses of **sympathy** given above. In the first sense, it is mostly used without a preposition, as in *He was very sympathetic, but he said he could do nothing to help me,* but it may be followed by **to** or **with**: *He was very sympathetic to me.* In the second sense, **sympathetic** is followed by **to** or **towards**: *I'm not sympathetic to his ideas; Some teachers are not sympathetic towards the new teaching methods.*

-t, -ed in verbs

A number of verbs have both a regularly formed past tense and past participle ending in **-ed** and a form ending in **-t**: *burned, burnt; leaped, leapt;* and similarly *dream, kneel, lean, learn, smell, spell, spill, spoil.* Note that in the **-t** forms, there are sometimes changes in the spelling and pronunciation of the base verb: *spill, spilled* but *spilt,* not **spillt; dream, dreamed* but *dreamt* (pronounced [*dremt*]). The regular **-ed** forms are usual in American English, the -t forms often preferred by speakers of British English, especially for the past participles, and particularly when the past participles are used as adjectives: *burnt cakes; spilt milk; a spoilt child.*

See also **knit** and **light**.

take place see **occur**.

tall, high

Tall and **high** are in some contexts interchangeable, but there are differences in meaning between the two words. **Tall** is applied to people and to animals and objects which have much greater height than breadth (e.g. giraffes, trees, buildings) and means 'having greater than average height in comparison to similar things': *a tall man; A giraffe is a very tall animal; A skyscraper is a tall building; He is very tall for his age.* In combination with a measurement, it means 'having a particular height' (not necessarily a great height), as in *He is six feet tall; The dwarf was only eighteen inches tall.*

High is used of things which rise to, or of people or things which are situated at, a great height: *high mountains; a high building; a high shelf; He was sitting on a high branch of a tall tree; There were three tall windows in one wall of the room and two small, high windows in the opposite wall.* Like **tall**, **high** may be used in the sense of 'having a particular height': *Those mountains are over six thousand feet high.*

than

When **than** is followed by a pronoun in comparative constructions, there is often uncertainty about the correct form of the pronoun to use. Should one, for example, say *He is taller than me* or *He
is taller than I*, *You love him more than me* or *You love him more than I*?

In informal English, the objective forms *me*, *him*, *her*, etc. are
always preferred, and to most people *I*, *we*, *she*, etc. would sound
inappropriately formal, even pompous or pretentious. Many
people would accept the use of objective forms of pronouns after
than in formal English also nowadays, especially in constructions in which there is no possibility of ambiguity or misunder-
standing: *He seems taller than me*; *He runs faster than me*. Constructions such as *You love him more than me* are, however, ambiguous
(this sentence could mean either 'You love him more than I love
him' or 'You love him more than you love me'). In such cases
many people, when speaking or writing in a formal style, would
use subjective forms of pronouns (*I*, *he*, etc.) when the pronoun
would have been the subject of the following verb (had it been
expressed), and the objective forms when the pronoun would
have been the object of the verb (had it been expressed): *You love
him more than I* would then mean 'You love him more than I do',
and *You love him more than me* would mean 'You love him more than
you love me'.

In order to make such sentences completely unambiguous, however, it is often better to add a verb to what follows **than**: *You love
him more than I do*; *You love him more than you do me.*

than what

An unnecessary **what** sometimes follows **than** in comparative
constructions, e.g. **You can do that better than what I can.* Such an
expression is not acceptable, and should be avoided. Only if
what means 'that which, the thing(s) which' can it correctly follow **than**. Compare the example given above with *Those are better
than what we saw in the shops yesterday*, in which the use of **what** (=
the things which) is entirely grammatical.

that

Many people think that the relative pronoun **that** (as in *the man
that I saw*) is informal, and that it should be replaced by **who** or
which in formal speech and writing. This is not the case at all:
that is as appropriate in formal contexts as it is in a more collo-

quial style of language, and is often much to be preferred as sounding much more natural than **which** or **who**. However, where the relative clause is separated from the rest of the sentence, by pauses in speech or commas in writing, only **who** or **which** may be used, never *****that**. Compare *The man that I saw suddenly turned and ran off* and *The man, whom I had seen the day before, suddenly turned and ran off.*

there is/are see **here/there is.**

they, them, their

One most annoying gap in English vocabulary is that created by the lack of a third person singular pronoun that does not state explicitly the sex of the person or persons referred to, as do *he, him, she, her*, etc. The lack of such a pronoun leads to some uncertainty as to the correct pronoun to choose to refer back to a male and female noun linked together (as in *Neither John nor Mary has finished his/his or her/their project yet*) or to an indefinite noun, pronoun, or adjective such as *a person, anyone, each, every, everyone, no-one, some* or *someone* which refers to individuals whose sex is not known or stated or who belong to a group which includes both males and females (as in *The teacher told the boys and girls in the class that each of them must finish his/his or her/their project by the end of the week*).

In the past, grammarians have recommended the use of *his, him*, etc. in such contexts, and this must still be considered correct today. However, many people dislike the use of an otherwise masculine pronoun to refer to males and females, but equally regard the more explicit *him and her, his and her* as very awkward and cumbersome. *Them, their*, etc. are therefore often used in such contexts instead of the *him, his*, etc. recommended by grammarians: *Has anyone lost their pencil?*; *Has everyone finished their project?* This is now acceptable to almost all speakers of English in informal contexts, and is increasingly common in formal speech and writing as well, though still disapproved of by some purists. There is no reason to avoid this use of *them, their*, etc. In choosing between *him, him and her, them*, and so on, one is free to follow one's own personal taste and preferences, according to what one thinks sounds best in a particular context.

till see **until.**

too see **also.**

top: on top see **above.**

toward, towards

Both forms of this preposition are correct, but the form with -*s* is preferred in British English, Americans preferring the form with no -*s*.

transpire

Transpire is often used, especially in formal contexts, as a substitute for **happen** or **occur**. Some people deprecate this use of **transpire**, which originally meant 'to leak out, become known gradually', but it has become so widespread that it must now be accepted as correct.

treble, triple

In the sense of 'three times as much', **treble** and **triple** may both be used as verbs, adverbs, and nouns. There is no difference in meaning but **treble** is the commoner of the two: *It doesn't matter what he offers you, I'll offer you treble*; *I'll offer you treble what he offers you*; *He trebled his earnings in just six months*. **Treble** and **triple** may both also be used as adjectives, but as adjectives they do differ slightly in meaning. **Treble** is commoner than **triple** in the sense of 'three times as much or as many': *treble scotch*. **Triple** is more frequently used than **treble** in the sense of 'of three kinds, parts, units, etc.', as in *They have the triple handicap of poverty, parental neglect and bad schooling*; *Round the prison they built a triple wall*; *the treble chance*.

trillion see million.

triple see treble.

try and, try to

In all contexts, **try** may be followed by the preposition **to** and an infinitive: *He tried to catch the ball*; *Will he try to talk to her?*; *He has been trying to see her for days but she's always out*. **Try and** is sometimes substituted for **try to**, but is subject to two important restrictions: it should not be used in formal speech and writing, and it must only be used when **try** is not modified by a suffix such as -*ing* or -*es*: *Do try and come to the party*; *I will try and come*; *He did try and come*; but not **He tried and came to the party*; **He was trying and coming to the party*.

turquoise

Many people are uncertain about how to pronounce this word, the modern spelling of which has been taken from French. There are in fact three common and equally acceptable pronunciations of this word: [*tûr′kwoiz*], [*tûr′koiz*], and , in partial imitation of the French pronunciation, [*tûr′kwäz*].

un- see **in-**.

unaware, unawares

Unaware is an adjective meaning 'not aware, not knowing': *I was unaware of the man's presence*; *She was unaware that the man was in the room.* **Unawares** is an adverb meaning 'unintentionally, without being aware of it', as in *She dropped her handkerchief unawares*, or 'unexpectedly, by surprise', as in the idiomatic expression **take/ catch someone unawares** (= to take someone by surprise, when they are not expecting it or prepared for it): *He tiptoed into the room and caught me unawares.* **Unaware** (with no *s*) may sometimes be seen used as an adverb, but most authorities recommend the distinction between **unaware** and **unawares** outlined above.

under, underneath see **below**.

unexceptional, unexceptionable

Unexceptional is a rather formal adjective meaning 'ordinary, not unusual or remarkable': *His book has been praised highly but it seems quite unexceptional to me.* It must not be confused with the equally formal adjective **unexceptionable**, which means 'about which there is nothing to object to or criticize' as in *His speech was unexceptionable*; *His book has been condemned as blasphemous by some critics, but his language seems quite unexceptionable to me.*

uninterested see **disinterested**.

unique

The adjective **unique** means 'being the only one of its kind, having no like or equal': *This vase is unique — there isn't another one like it in the world*; *a comedian with a unique sense of timing.* It follows from the meaning of the word that **unique** is a 'yes or no' term, not a 'more or less' term: either something is unique or it isn't, it cannot be *more unique, *very unique, *fairly unique or *slightly unique. In informal language, **unique** is quite frequently used to mean 'rare, unusual', often modified by adverbs such as *more, fairly*, etc.: *He's got a pretty unique job*; *This is a rather unique picture.* This use of the word is not generally considered correct, and must certainly be avoided in careful, formal speech and writing.

unlike see **like**.

unreadable see **illegible**.

until, till

These two words are synonymous and interchangeable, but **until** is found more often than **till** at the beginning of a sentence: *I'll wait until/till he arrives*; *Until he arrives, we won't know why he wants to see us*. Note the spelling of **until** (with one *l*) and **till** (with a double *l*).

upon

Upon means the same as **on**, but is now generally used only in formal or literary contexts. Apart from the obligatory use of **upon** in a few idioms such as **upon my word** and **once upon a time**, **on** is nearly always to be preferred.

upward, upwards

Upward and **upwards** may both be used as adverbs: *He was lying on the floor face upwards*; *The path led upward into the mountains*. The form with *s* is commoner in British English, and the form without *s* in American English.

As an adjective, only **upward** is correct: *an upward movement*. **Upward**, or **upwards**, **of** means 'more than': *There were upwards of a hundred people at the meeting*.

use, usage

These two nouns are sometimes confused with each other. **Use** refers to the act of using something or the purpose for which it is used: *The use of force cannot be justified*; *That is an incorrect use of the word*; *This little lamp has many uses*. **Usage**, on the other hand, means 'the manner of using or being used', as in *These tools have been subjected to rough usage*, or 'custom or habit, especially with regard to the generally accepted rules of language': *We must be aware of ancient traditions and usages*; *This book is a guide to modern English usage*.

used to

There is often uncertainty about the correct negative forms of this phrase. The following are all acceptable: *He used not to do it*; *He didn't use to do it*; *He usen't to do it*; *He usedn't to do it*. Similarly, the following question forms are all unexceptionable: *Did he use/used to do it?*; *Didn't he use /used to do it?*; *Used he to do it?*; *Used he not to do it?*; *Usen't he to do it?*; *Usedn't he to do it?* The form *Used he not to do it?* is appropriate only in very formal contexts; the other forms may be used informally; and in formal speech and writing the best forms to use are *He used not to do it*, *Used he to do it?*, and *Didn't he use to do it?*

vengeance see **avenge.**

verbal see **oral.**

very, much

Very is used to qualify ordinary adjectives (e.g. *dark, big, silly*): *He is very tall*; *a very foolish little boy*. **Much** and **greatly** are used to qualify past participles (verb-forms ending in *-ed* or sometimes *-t* or *-n*), even when these are used as adjectives: *His house has been much admired*; *He has a very beautiful and much admired house*; *The problems have been greatly exaggerated*; *Diamonds are much sought after*; *This is a highly praised work of art.*

There are, however, a few past participles which have now lost their verbal force and are treated as ordinary adjectives. These must be qualified by **very**, not **much**: *I am very tired*; *We were very pleased to see him*; *He is very interested in stamps*. There is, unfortunately, no clear, simple, and hard-and-fast rule which can be given to help one to decide which words belong to this adjectival category and which do not, but here are a few guidelines which may help:

  1. If the word is followed by the preposition **by**, it is probably being used as a verb; if by some other preposition, it is probably an adjective: *I was very annoyed with him* (adjective) but *I was annoyed by his constant interruptions* (verb); *He seemed very harassed* (adjective) but *The soldiers retreated, much harassed by the enemy.*

  2. If the word refers to a state rather than to an action, occurrence, or sudden feeling, it is probably an adjective rather than a verb: *I was feeling very irritated with him* (state) but *I was irritated by his persistent interruptions* (repeated action).

  3. If the word refers to people's expressions, faces, movements, etc. rather than to the people themselves, it is an adjective, not a verb: *He had a very amused expression on his face.*

virus see **bacterium.**

wait, await

The verb **wait** is never followed by an object: *I'll wait until you come* is correct, but not **I'll wait your arrival*. Before an object, one must say **wait for**: *I'll wait for you*; *I'll wait for the train to arrive*. **Await** is a rather formal synonym of 'wait for', and must always be followed by an object: *I'm awaiting the arrival of the train*: *We are awaiting your instructions*; but not **I'll await until you come.*

Await also means 'to be in store for, be waiting for': *A warm wel-*

come awaits you at this church on Sunday. In this sense, it cannot be replaced by **wait for**.

To **wait on** means 'to serve': *Waiters wait on tables*; *The servants had to wait on their master day and night.*

wake, waken, awake, awaken

These four verbs are virtually synonymous and are interchangeable in most contexts. **Wake** is the most commonly used of the four. Its past tense is usually **woke** (but **waked** is also acceptable, though rather rare) and its past participle is **woken** (but **waked** is again permissible): *He woke to find that it was snowing*; *He went and woke the others.* The past tense and past participle of **waken** are **wakened**: *Have you wakened the children?*; *I wakened at seven o'clock.* The past tense of **awake** is usually **awoke** (rarely **awaked**) and the past participle **awaked** or **awoken**. **Awaken**, like **waken**, has a regularly-formed past tense and past participle, **awakened**.

Wake may be followed by **up** (*I woke up at seven o'clock*) and **waken** sometimes is; **awake** and **awaken** are never followed by **up**.

weights and measures

Note that in compound adjectives denoting weights and measures, such as *two-foot*, the noun forming the second part of the compound is always in the singular: *a six-foot plank of wood*; *a three-pound chicken*; *a ten-gallon drum*. However, in phrases denoting weights and measures, the noun must be plural: *This plank is six feet long*, not *six foot long; *This chicken weighs three pounds*, not *three pound.

what

There is sometimes some uncertainty about whether to follow **what** by a singular or plural verb. The rule is, however, very simple: when **what** means 'that which', it is singular and must be followed by a singular verb; when it means 'those which', it is plural and must be followed by a plural verb. The following examples show the correct constructions: *What I need is a cup of tea*; *They looked through all their books and what they didn't need were sold at a jumble sale.* Sometimes, when a verb following a singular **what** is followed by a plural noun, the verb is made plural to agree with the plural noun: **What we need are a few sticks and some string.* This is not correct, as the subject of the verb is **what**, a singular pronoun. The sentence should read *What we need is a few sticks and some string.* **What** must never be substituted for **who**, **which** or **that** in relative clauses. Expressions like **the man what I saw yesterday*, or *the

chairs what were in the shop are not correct standard English.
See also **which**; **than what.**

which, what

Which and **what** may both be used as interrogative adjectives
(i.e. to ask questions about a choice or selection) but they are not
interchangeable: **which** implies choice from a limited number of
things, whereas **what** is used when the choice is unlimited.
See also **whose.**

who, whom

Strictly speaking, **who** is a subject pronoun, **whom** an objective
form, comparable to **he** and **him**, **I** and **me**, etc. The following
examples show the correct constructions: *Who told you that?*; *The
man who was standing at the bus stop turned and ran off*; *Whom should we
send?*; *To whom is the letter addressed?* However, in modern English,
whom is generally replaced by **who** when it stands at the beginning of a sentence or clause: *Who should we send?*; *Who is the letter
addressed to?*; *I don't know who it is addressed to*. Although deprecated
by some people, this is generally acceptable to most speakers of
English in informal contexts, and is only to be avoided in the
most careful and formal speech and writing.

Care must be taken not to substitute **whom** for **who** when **who**
is the subject of a following verb. In **the man whom I said would be
waiting for us*, **whom** should in fact be **who**, as it is not the object
of *said* but the subject of *would be waiting*. This becomes clearer if,
as a test, one removes the *I said*: *the man who would be waiting for us*.
A similar test would lead to the correction of the same error in
*the man whom I hear was in charge of the investigation and **the little girl
whom I was informed won first prize in the competition.*

wholly

Note the spelling of this adverb. Unlike most adverbs formed
from adjectives ending in a silent *e*, **wholly** drops the *e* of **whole**
before the *-ly* is added.

whom see who.

whose, of which

Note the correct spelling of **whose**. **Who's** does not mean 'of
whom', but 'who is' or 'who has'.

Whose is correctly used to mean 'of whom' and 'of which': *the boy
whose father is a policeman*; *the book whose pages are torn*. **Of which**
may also be used of things, as in *the book, the pages of which are torn*,
but **whose** is now generally preferred.

wide

When **who** is linked with **else**, **who else's** is more usual than **whose else**.

wide see **broad**.

will see **shall**.

would see **should**.

-xion see **-ction**.